9/13

FATHER OF
ART PHOTOGRAPHY

O. G. Rejlander
1813-1875

THE TWO WAYS OF LIFE (1857)

(above) Carte-de-visite copy of probable first version (1) (courtesy Edinburgh Photographic Society)

(below) Probable later version (2) from original print (courtesy Permanent Collection, Royal Photographic Society)

FATHER OF ART PHOTOGRAPHY

O. G. Rejlander
1813-1875

Edgar Yoxall Jones

NEW YORK GRAPHIC SOCIETY LTD
Greenwich, Connecticut

International Standard Book Number
0-8212-0598-6

Library of Congress Catalog Card Number
73-89945

First published in Great Britain 1973 by
David & Charles (Holdings) Ltd

Published in the United States and Canada
by New York Graphic Society Ltd.
Greenwich, Connecticut 06830

Printed in Great Britain

CONTENTS

LIST OF ILLUSTRATIONS

KEY TO FRONTISPIECE

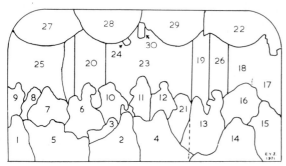

Version 1

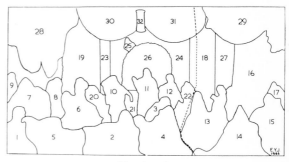

Version 2

Key to the three known* copies of *The Two Ways of Life*, numbered in the probable order of printing, following (as far as possible) Rejlander's own description. Version 1 is copied from what appears to be a second generation copy, and in places the exact position of the joins is a matter of conjecture.

1 THE OLD HAG Probably inspired by the old brothel-keeper in George Reynolds' *The Mysteries of London* (1846).

2 A BACCHANTE Nude holding a stein in her left hand and a pewter mug in her right.

3 MURDER Sited differently in each version.

4 PENITENCE There are two separate versions of this model. In her right hand the model holds an anchor, the emblem of Hope. A subsidiary title for *The Two Ways of Life* was *Hope in Repentance*.

5 THE IDLE GROUP The left-hand figure is probably the same as the model shown in profile in 4.

6 THE SIRENS Foremost figure probably veiled model in 4.

7 THE GAMBLERS The left-hand character is probably John Coleman; there is some resemblance about the nose. The right-hand figure may be Rejlander himself.

8 COMPLICITY Probably the same pair as in 6.

9 THE PINIONED MAN

10 THE WAYWARD YOUTH The drooping left hand may have been intended to facilitate a join-up with another model.

11 THE SAGE This character is different in both versions.

12 THE RIGHTEOUS YOUTH In version 2 the right hand is not actually being grasped by the Sage.

13 THE RELIGIOUS GROUP Veiled figure holding a cross, and the semi-nude penitent appear to be professional models. The girl reading a book resembles one of the models in *Fortune-telling*.

14 GOOD WORKS

15 MENTAL APPLICATION There are indications that the student's profile was printed in separately.

16 (version 1) INDUSTRIOUS GROUP This pseudo-classical group has been closely vignetted, and does not appear to have been posed in front of the alcove.

16 (version 2) INDUSTRIOUS GROUP The shadow of the woman's upraised arm on the wall behind suggests that this group was in fact posed in front of the alcove; though whether this was real, or a painted back-drop, cannot be determined.

17 MARRIED LIFE One of the groups whose image was photographed in a mirror to obtain the correct perspective.

18 (version 1) ALCOVE

18 (version 2) COLUMN Note join between both printing papers down left-hand edge. This is an original print, and the blemishes are due to the effects of time.

19 (version 1) COLUMN

20 (version 1) and 19 (version 2) COLUMN ENCIRCLED WITH VINE

20 (version 2) STONE LIONESS AND STEPS

21 (version 1) STONE LION The Fifth Commandment, 'Honour thy father, and thy mother, etc' is inscribed on the pedestal.

21 (version 2) STEPS

22 (version 1) and 29 (version 2) CURTAINS WITH FRINGE

22 (version 2) STONE LION Join cuts diagonally across pedestal.

23 (version 1), 24 and 26 (version 2) RUSTIC ARCH WITH LANDSCAPE It is difficult to decide whether or not the arch and background are two separate photographs.

24 (version 1) and 25 (version 2) SPECTRAL MOTHER

25 and 26 (version 1) CURTAINS

27 (version 2) CURTAINS

27, 28, 29 (version 1), 28, 29, 30, 31 (version 2) DRAPES

30 (version 1) and 32 (version 2) HOURGLASS

*A variant of version 1 is in the Permanent Collection of the Royal Photographic Society, London, in which the figure of REPENTANCE is the same as in version 2. Also the Fifth Commandment is absent from the pedestal, and there are other slight differences.

PREFACE

Whenever Rejlander is mentioned, that extraordinary photomontage *The Two Ways of Life* comes to mind, with its moral and its nudes. This study has not been neglected by historians of the camera, but the rest of his work is little known; and no attempt has been made since his death nearly a century ago to illustrate the story of this remarkable Swede. An eccentric and part-genius, whose photographs were the centre of attraction wherever they were shown, he counted the Prince Consort and Lewis Carroll amongst his friends and admirers.

During his photographic career Rejlander earned a modest living taking photographic studies for artists. In evidence of his own training in art these showed the unmistakable influence of the old masters, whether of a Raphael or a Jan Steen, and a distinct partiality for allegory. But within him the *real* struggled with the *ideal*, and one observes his attempts at candid photography decades before it became technically possible. He wanted expression and life, and abhorred the rigidly pleasant, Sunday-best pose. But the wet-plate was too slow for him so he induced expression in his sitters, gesticulating like a genial Svengali while the long exposure was being counted away. Some of his pictures reveal a deep, surrealistic imagination interesting to a psycho-analyst.

Here are illustrated examples of Rejlander's early tableaux and genre, compositions, allegory, and studies of the ideal, compared (where possible) with contemporary comment. Sometimes the comment, or a faded copy, is all that remains, for many of the originals have disappeared. His achievements relate to an early period in photographic history, and to an archaic process, but this does not affect the timeless, human quality of his pictures; and the obtrusion of an out-of-focus door-handle is forgivable when the expression of the sitter has been caught so splendidly.

I was concerned to seek out those of Rejlander's studios which still remained, and in particular the one in Darlington Street, Wolverhampton, where he had taken his early studies, including those for *The Two Ways of Life*. My detective work was first conducted by correspondence, at a time when redevelopment was taking place in the town. A friend kindly photographed both sides of the street, and from these pictures I deduced which one among the remaining houses could have been Rejlander's studio. When I arrived there a month later it had been demolished. Afterwards it was confirmed that it had been the place: no 42.

The Albert Mansions studio survives by chance, for the bombs rained around it during the Blitz. The room where the Solar Club group was taken is now divided into offices, and the great window (probably a bomb casualty) replaced with smaller panes. A floor has been added above, obliterating the skylight; but one still can recognise the skirting board, and stonework outside the arched window in *An Interesting Sight*.

Rejlander has been an elusive quarry, and there is still much to discover about him. I had hoped to penetrate his domestic establishment with the aid of the 1851 census. Alas, the Rejlander house was vacant! Nevertheless, there was another chance in 1861. But again, while there are many returns for Wolverhampton, there is a blank space beside no 42, and at some later date the following comment had been entered: 'This was left at Mr. Rejlander's Home but he was on a journey.'

PROLOGUE

Regent Street, London, in the year 1853—a promenade of elegance and fashion: the crowd surges this way and that, admiring the latest Paris fashions, coming and going from the haberdashers and the jewellers, or inspecting the displays of daguerreotype portraits which glisten in photographers' doorways.

Seeking Henneman's studio, there hurries into the scene a sandy-haired, blue-eyed Swede, Oscar Gustav Rejlander, garbed as an artist. Finding the place he rapidly explains to the expert that he wishes to learn photography—and could he have all the lessons there and then, please, for he must catch the night train home to Wolverhampton.

Henneman is taken aback, but promises to do his best, and soon the artist is scribbling procedures and formulas which are as intelligible as Greek to him. He poses a sitter—no novelty—but in the darkroom, its twilight redolent of sickly odours, he discovers how easy it is to spill chemicals and fumble with large glass plates. Rejlander soon realises how much there is to learn.[1]

In daguerreotype portraiture the image lay upon the surface of a small silver tablet which was treated as a precious keepsake, and mounted in a plush-lined morocco case, or a papier-mâché simulacrum of Birmingham manufacture. It was admired for its fine detail; but it was unique and did not lend itself to reproduction, nor was it cheap. In England it was patronised mainly by the middle and upper classes, who approached the camera self-consciously and with dignity, dressed in their Sunday best, wearing that 'rigidly pleasant' expression which became a tradition in photographic portraiture, and which has not entirely died out to this day. But at that period the expression was also conditioned by the weather, for on a dull day the exposure could last as long as a minute, and there are few sitters who can freeze a smile for that time.

The calotype—the original negative/positive process—was not a success in commercial portraiture. Prints were contact printed from a paper negative; but the texture sometimes obtruded, preventing crisp detail. But it was superior for landscape and topographic work, yielding prints which resembled mezzotints in their warmth of tone. Its advantage over the rival process lay in the facility with which it could be reproduced.

By 1853 the daguerreotype patent had expired, Fox Talbot was seeking an extension for his calotype patent, and a third contender—the collodion, or wet-plate—had made its appearance. This also was a negative/positive process, the details of which had been published in England by Scott Archer two years previously. Its manipulation required considerable dexterity, and there were whole families of defects which could ruin a negative. But it had three incomparable virtues: exposures were minimal by comparison with the earlier processes; the collodion image was virtually grainless; and the image could be processed to yield either a negative or a positive.

For a short time Fox Talbot hindered the early exploitation of the wet-plate, claiming that it infringed his patent. Apart from this check, the invention rapidly widened interest in photography, and there was a widespread demand for instruction. Manuals were purchased together with strange and noxious chemicals, cellars became darkrooms, and there were sundry explosions.

Shortly before Rejlander's hurried visit, two reporters from Dickens's family journal, *Household Words*, visited Henneman's establishment to describe the collodion process:

'He (Henneman) took a square of glass, cleaned

it very perfectly, then holding it up by one corner with the left hand, he poured over the centre of the glass some collodion, which is, as most people know, gun-cotton dissolved in ether. By a few movements of the left hand, which appear easy, but are acquired with trouble, the collodion was caused to flow into an even coat over the surface of the glass, and the excess was poured off at another corner. To do this by a few left-handed movements without causing any ripples on the collodion adhering to the glass is really very difficult. This done, the plate was left till the ether had almost evaporated, and deposited a film of gun-cotton—evenly over the glass. The glass, before it was yet quite dry, was plunged carefully into a pan or bath, containing a solution of nitrate of silver. In about two minutes it was taken out, and ready for the camera.'

A portrait was taken, and after removal from the dark-slide, the plate 'was dipped into another bath (of pyrogallic acid) and the impression soon became apparent. To bring it out with greater force (the negative) was then dipped into a second and much weaker bath of nitrate of silver.' This was the essence of the wet-plate process, although no mention is made of printing paper, which also was sensitised by the photographer himself.[2]

A notable event in early photography was the famous soirée at the Society of Arts, London, in December 1852. This was the first comprehensive exhibition of photography and it initiated the Photographic Society of London (later the 'Royal'), founded in the following year. One of its founders, Roger Fenton—yet to make photographic history in the Crimea—called upon artists to reject the view that the camera was their rival. It was a creative instrument, he said, which left the artist 'the power of judgement, the play of fancy, and the power of invention'. He inquired, 'What practical use has been made of it in the artist's studio? Those natural attitudes of the human form which come unbidden—is there any pencil so rapid that it can depict them before meaning has departed from the pose?'[3]

In 1852, the answer was, none.

Rejlander's afternoon of instruction was over. Three hours for the calotype, and half an hour for the wet-plate. On the train his mind must have reeled. Years later, when he was famous, he was to remark somewhat ruefully, 'I was too clever. It would have saved me a year of trouble and expense had I attended carefully to the rudiments of the art for a month.'[4]

WOLVERHAMPTON

Little is known of Rejlander's early life. It is probable that he was born in Sweden, though his actual birthplace has yet to be traced.[1] When he died on 18 January 1875 his death certificate gave his age as 61. Yet pictures taken in 1871—admittedly while he was sickening for diabetes—suggest that he was older. His obituarists state that his father was an officer in the Swedish Army,[2] but an extensive search has not revealed a single officer of this name—only a 'Rylander', none of whose children were named Oscar Gustav.[3]

From early youth he studied painting, eventually satisfying his desire to study in Rome, where he supported himself by portraiture, copying the old masters, and lithography. He is believed also to have visited Spain, 'afterwards returning to Rome [where] he met with a romantic love adventure resulting in his visiting England',[4] which became the country of his adoption. Mary, his wife, was probably English. She was comely, knew how to pose either in costume or in the nude, and was probably illiterate.

In 1841, Rejlander was established in Lincoln, and there exists a charcoal sketch of an election scene which he made from his rooms on Castle Hill;[5] and there also he was initiated into Freemasonry.[6]

By 1846 the Rejlanders had moved to Wolverhampton, a workaday town noted for its locks, safes, and japanned and papier-mâché ware. On the borders of the notorious Black Country, it must have seemed a long way from Rome with its ancient churches and monuments, its fireworks bursting in the darkness over St Angelo, and its dark-eyed beauties waiting on the Spanish Steps to catch the artist's eye.[7]

Why Wolverhampton? Probably for domestic reasons, for Mary's sister and her husband may

42 Darlington Street, Wolverhampton, Rejlander's house and studio 1845?-62. Photographed July 1966, shortly before demolition. (Courtesy Mr John Underwood)

have resided in the town a few years later.[8] But it is possible that Rejlander had been attracted to Waltons, makers of papier-mâché articles, who, in 1846 had advertised widely for artists to embellish their trays and knick-knacks[9]—now collectors' pieces.

Whether or not Rejlander ever painted centre-pieces for a living, it is known that he exhibited a portrait of a young girl, entitled *'Oh yes! Oh yes! Oh yes!'* at the Royal Academy of 1848.[10] His home and studio was on Darlington Street (later numbered 42), near what is now Art Street, opposite open ground where fairs and circuses were held on high days and holidays.

Culturally, Wolverhampton was a backwater. What culture there was centred around the bookshop of William Parke, who was also part-owner of the *Wolverhampton Chronicle*.[11] Parke befriended the Swedish artist, introduced sitters to him, and eventually provided the means whereby he was instructed in photography. Among his friends was a young clergyman with an interest in photography, Rev Edward Bradley ('Cuthbert Bede'), who was also a contributor of cartoons to *Punch*, and Christmas articles to the *Illustrated London News*. Probably at Parke's instigation, Bede described a portrait session in what was undoubtedly Rejlander's studio, about the summer of 1853:

'The operator was a Swede,' he wrote, 'light-haired, red mustachioed, and with a fez. I sat at my ease on a couch, backed by a screen of black velvet. The good-natured operator, in the best English he could muster, explained to me the nature of the process (even taking me into his dark den of magic), and remarked with great truth, "When beebles do come for vaat you call bortraits, dey most not dink dey are in de leetle rum by demself, bot dey most dink dat all de world look at dem! dat dey are having deir bortraits bainted before a crowd, oh! so vast! dat dey are on the stage of de theatre, wid den dousand beebles all a-looking at dem, and not shot up here in de leetle rum, by demself. Now, sare! gompose your features for de bortrait: and when I say 'Now!' de operation will gommence." '[12]

Rejlander's breezy and engaging character comes through, as well as his childlike trust and enthusiasm. There is no evidence that he was ever on the stage, but 'the stage of de theatre' may be significant.

He is listed as an artist in the local directories of 1847, 1849 and 1851. Curiously, his house was vacant during the 1851 census, but he

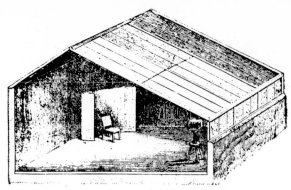

Fig 1 Ridge-roof studio similar to Rejlander's at 42 Darlington Street, Wolverhampton

visited the Great Exhibition in Hyde Park in that year and commented upon its photographic exhibits: 'What I saw,' he said, 'proved as evanescent as looking at myself in a glass, out of sight out of mind. They were all Daguerreotypes.' He had also seen some 'reddish landscapes at Ackermann's, in Regent Street', [calotypes] which had left no lasting impression. But in Rome in the following year he changed his opinion regarding the value of photography, and determined to learn the technique as soon as he returned to England.

'My view at this period,' he recounted, 'to the best of my recollection, did not extend further than showing me the usefulness of photography in enabling me to take children's portraits, in aid of painting, and for studies for foregrounds in landscapes.'

'It is curious to notice how frequently trifles decide some men's actions. What really hurried me forward was my having seen the photograph of a gentleman, and the fold of his coat sleeve was just the very thing I required for a portrait I was then painting at home, and could not please myself on this particular point. My sitter had not time or inclination to sit for it; my lay figure was too thin (I soon sold that); but this was just "like life!"'[13]

'Now,' said he, seeing the merits of photo-

12

graphy, 'I shall get all I want.' And impatiently (and thanks to William Parke)[14] he took all the lessons at once, 'to turn out as a ready-made photographer the next day'.

In those days, when every photographer was also an experimentalist, how much harder it was for the beginner. Although some excellent instruction manuals were available, it was usual to perfect one's own variations of the wet-plate technique—hindered, as a rule, by unreliable chemicals.

Rejlander soon discovered that his prints faded. 'I felt as if I were only writing on sand,' he said, and felt like giving it up.[15] One cause was inadequate washing. The Rejlander household shared a pump with their next-door neighbour. When every gallon was carried indoors by the bucketful one understands why print washing was sometimes minimal.

The stone-laying ceremony of the Wolverhampton School of Art on Darlington Street took place on a wet afternoon in June 1853. The proceedings began with a prayer, followed by a rending crash as the floor gave way, precipitating the mayor and corporation into the vault below; but no one was seriously hurt.[16] Charles Mander, JP, manufacturer of papier-mâché ware, and honorary secretary of the school, was a keen amateur photographer.[17] This common interest in art and photography undoubtedly brought him into contact with Rejlander, who shortly joined the school management committee.[18]

Features of most mid-Victorian middle-class parlours were the piano, the scrap-book, and the portfolio which may have contained Doyle's *Punch* cartoons, Leech's sporting prints, and Cruikshank's cautionary caricatures together with the sentimental engravings of Landseer, Mulready, or Frith. During the fifties calotype views also became available, though expensive, for there was no successful photo-engraving process at that time. Then Rejlander conceived the possibilities of photographic genre. The domestic tableaux of the Dutch masters came to his mind: the doctor and the love-sick girl; the gnarled grandfather with the sleeping child; the beaming drunkard and the ale-wife.

And the models? As he glanced out of his window he saw the muffin-man conversing with the pretty maidservant; the little potman from the Darlington Arms (no doubt); thick sinewed women carrying laundry baskets—and children everywhere. Here, in his imagination, lay the Spanish Steps.

He was an actor-manager with an instinct for generally casting the right character in the right part. He selected his 'performers' from amongst his friends, but occasionally accosted a photogenic stranger in the street. An expressive face triggered his imagination, and soon he would be fitting a story to it. The question was frequently asked—'How does Mr Rejlander get such models, and hire such expressions which are beyond the reach of money?'

In the studio the sitter's self-consciousness evaporated as the voluble Swede, gesticulating and acting the part himself, inspired his model until the expression he sought blossomed naturally and without effort.

But the technical difficulties were formidable. To catch an expression by electronic flash requires no great skill, but to induce it to remain fixed and natural while the lens cap was off for ten, eleven or twelve seconds (according to the weather) demanded almost hypnotic gifts. Or, waiting with his hand on the lens cap, waiting intently for the expression, he would forget that the plate was rapidly losing sensitivity. A fresh plate would be at hand, but changing it might break the spell.

Photographic societies were springing up in all the large cities, and their annual exhibitions were open to all-comers. These were a form of advertising for the professional, and the pictures were priced, a percentage accruing to the society. Reports were then printed in the local press.

Rejlander's work soon aroused comment: 'the expressions—is astonishing'; it was remarked, 'the very thought of each individual is fully expressed in his face'.[19] His child studies, *Perception*, *The Young Philosopher*, and *Early Contemplation*—unique at that time—were considered 'beautiful as those of Della Robbia, Flamingo, or Raphael'.[20] His study, *After Raphael's Sistine Madonna*, depicts two flesh and blood cherubs. They are minus wings and not as chubby, nor as dreamy as Raphael's, but still very charming.

'His scenes are all pictures,' wrote a critic, 'well thought out, most ingenious in their subjects, and most wonderful in their truth and exactness of expression. His models are sometimes ill-chosen, but in this matter an artist is limited in choice.'[21]

And 'the wonderfully clever studies by Rejlander,' commented another, 'who can tell how much labour these may have cost the artist? Let not the tyro go home and fancy he can do the like without much thought and trouble.'[22]

Rejlander claimed it was hard enough to pose a single figure, let alone a group. Yet in *Fortune-Telling*, for instance, each figure is steady and natural—evidence of painstaking rehearsal.

A picture of which only the description survives shows an inventive use of characters in windows. It was 'a back-garden view, in which an entire household was seen stirred to its very depths by a most common but interesting event: the maid and manservant are making warm love outside the door of the back kitchen. From the windows above children peer down, from another window the grandmother, and at a french window the master and mistress are stealing forth to detect the culprits. Rejlander's mother-in-law, sister-in-law and her husband, himself and child, his maidservant and his wife, were the actors in this little comedy.—To balance the composition, a rocking-horse was put to admirable use.'[23]

PHOTOGRAPHS by O. G. REJLANDER.
FIFTY of his best mounted on Cardboard, and in a Portfolio (22 inches by 18), price £12 12s.—For further particulars apply to O. G REJLANDER, Wolverhampton.

Fig 2 Rejlander's advertisement in the Illustrated London News, *7 February 1857*

These domestic scenes were sold either direct or through art dealers or bookshops. Joseph Hogarth, of 5 Haymarket, was probably his London agent; and in Birmingham, E. Beckingham, chemist, of Great Hampton Street.[24] He may also have advertised in the press; an insertion appeared in the *Illustrated London News* in February 1857.

No landscapes appear to have survived, though he may not have taken many. There were photographs of *Lichfield Cathedral*, *Moseley Old Hall*, and the Severn Bridge at *Bridgenorth*—places within easy reach by railway. An early picture of a market place was examined with sober interest: 'We look with the greatest pleasure at his *Market*, in which persons, horses, and carts are rendered most clearly, thus testifying to the extreme rapidity of their execution.'[25]

'*You look as well as ever you did*' was pure sentiment, 'a pleasant morsel of domestic poetry, unaffected and touching...The husband is complimenting the old wife with a rustic courtliness very graceful and fond. The kindly old woman—smilingly denies the flattery. Like all Mr Rejlander's scenes, this picture seems a glimpse of real nature, and not a laborious composition of models and furniture.'[26]

This is an oblique reference to Lake Price, another artist-cum-photographer, whose preference was for the 'historical'; his characters carousing heavily in suits of armour like stage supernumeraries.

The *Art Journal* at first made no distinction between the studies of Lake Price and Rejlander, remarking: 'They are wonderfully clever, but after all they are but images of actors posed for the occasion; they all want life, expression, passion. Passion they have none, and yet these pictures tell a pleasant tale. We doubt the propriety of attempting to rival the historical painter—Such pictures as these will have a tendency to lower the appreciation of Art in the eyes of the public, and unfit them for receiving the full impression intended by the artist's production. They are excellent of their kind, but our love of High Art leads us to desire to see not too many of this class of subjects.'[27]

Rejlander believed that the invention of photography would make painters better artists and more careful draughtsmen. Of Titian's *Venus and Adonis*, he observed that 'Venus had her head turned in a manner that no female could turn it and at the same time show so much of her back. Her right leg also is too long. I have proved the correctness of this opinion by photography with variously-shaped female models. In *Peace and War*, by Reubens, the back of the female with the basket is painted from a male, as proved by the same test.'[28] *After Raphael's Sistine Madonna* is an example for comparison with the original.

At quite an early stage, Rejlander was experimenting with lighting to reduce exposure, and to accentuate texture and outline. The old man playing cat's-cradle with a little boy (*Play*), was taken in full, harsh sunlight in an attempt to 'stop' action. *Old English Oak* is side lit; and in *The Flycatcher*, the boy's face is lit by reflected light.

Rejlander's models reappear from time to time in his domestic tableaux, and it is likely that they were friends or in-laws. Even when the original photograph is lost, as in '*A young person wants to see your, Sir*', one can mentally supply the missing characters: 'A young rake is reclining on a sofa, when the old housekeeper announces a young woman with a suspicious baby. The three independent expressions are a good combination: the *quandom* lover, careless, surprised, indifferent; the old woman who points with her thumb, jerking contemptuously and accusingly back; and the girl, who, half angry, removes the handkerchief from the baby's face. The detail is marvellously good.'[29]

In September 1856, Rejlander, a leading light in the 'Bachelors'—a society whose aims appear to have been mainly convivial—announced a 'bespeak' at the Theatre Royal, Wolverhampton, on behalf of his friend John Coleman, 'for the great talent and ability he has displayed as a Dramatic Artist and Manager'.[30] The *Chronicle* subsequently reported that 'our expectations were realised'.

Considering this friendly association with Coleman, it is not surprising that several of Rejlander's pictures reflect the footlights; nor is it improbable that Coleman and members of his company posed in them. *Belphegor*, which Coleman had recently introduced to the British public at Coventry, was performed at the Theatre Royal, Wolverhampton, on 22 January 1855. Rejlander's photograph of him in the name part was described as 'exquisitely executed—with an old-master depth and beautiful modulation of shade and tone'.[31]

Richelieu, also in Coleman's repertoire, 'not so thin-faced and aquiline as he really was when he wore the red hat and gloves, is full of angry command and strong passion...'

'The *Man and Actor* are contrasting pictures. The one is a laughing orator, frank, coarse, and hearty, swaying a roll of paper and addressing a merry audience; the other is a sour, sanctimonious preacher, all starch and buckram, Maworm all over, with an unpliable fanatical hypocritical face...'[32]

'*An Actor's Day-Dream* is as good as a new novel...It represents a well-dressed man in a tightly-buttoned close-fitting frock coat, with one hand in the breast of it, leaning in a half doze against the portico pillar of a London theatre;

15

the hand is raised, giving the gesture of a moment's thought. To the left of him you see his dream: there he is again, coming in as Hamlet, with one leg bare, listening, with his hand to his ear, to the applause that fills the house—the noise that is his food, and of which he dreams day and night.'[33]

The latter picture is interesting for two reasons: first, the subject may have been suggested by Coleman himself, whose own affairs had vacillated between warm encouragement and chill poverty;[34] and secondly, because it was a composition photograph.

A composition photograph was a print whose component parts had been printed-in separately from two or more negatives, and it originated as a means of overcoming the tiresome optical and chemical limitations of the early collodion process. Stopping down to increase depth of focus was little used in group photography, for it increased exposure beyond practical limits. Using this method, sitters who had moved during exposure, or were unsharp, could be re-photographed (at the same distance from the camera) and the masked-out image would be printed-in where an appropriate space had been left on the sensitised paper.

Very soon, Rejlander saw that it also had aesthetic possibilities, and he began to pose studies which conformed in size, tone, lighting, and perspective to a pre-determined sketch or cartoon. The negatives were printed by contact, the edge of each group or figure being skilfully vignetted where it joined its neighbour. In theory, the method broadened the scope of photography at that time, but it required an artist to make it work. Considering Rejlander's background as a painter, it is understandable that he should attempt to emulate painting in photographic terms.

The process was incredibly laborious and time-consuming, but there must have been an aesthetic pleasure in watching the picture take form; each figure fitting into its appointed place; sensing the light sinking into the emulsion; and playing sunbeams over those parts which needed further darkening. But if the paper slipped and a figure went awry, or if a negative was not printed deeply enough, there was nothing to do but to start all over again.

It cannot be determined whether Rejlander discovered the principle of composition printing for himself, or whether he was aware of Berwick and Annan's combination print exhibited at the British Association in 1855;[35] but he was undoubtedly the first to grasp its creative possibilities, and many photographers were infected with his enthusiasm.

His first composition, *Groupe Printed from Three Negatives*, was exhibited in December 1855. This may also have been entitled *Canal Boys*, 'a most artistic group—rough and picturesque',[36] which depicted a group of canal boys with their donkey. The stolid bargees may have held their poses, but it is doubtful whether the donkey's head would have remained still, so it is likely that several pictures were taken, the most successful being printed-in.

In '*Drat the East Wind!*' photographers may have wondered how the young lady in the background reading a paper came to be as clear and sharp as the old lady rubbing her rheumaticky knees in the foreground. The old lady's light dress stands out against the adjoining dark area, concealing the join. In these circumstances the composition print was most successful; but where two light areas overlapped there would be a dark fringe because the exposure was doubled.

For over a century, Rejlander's massive composition *The Two Ways of Life* has been discussed by historians of the camera. The earlier ones marvelled at it as a photographic *tour de force*. More recently it has been brushed aside as a freak—a chimera, executed by an eccentric with a religious twist. Actually, Rejlander felt that he had hit upon a method of bringing photography closer to the technique of the painter, and *The Two Ways of Life* was the apotheosis of this belief.

Rejlander's election to the Photographic Society of London was noted in the *Photographic Journal* for 22 December 1856. In the same number was a letter from the secretary of the forthcoming Manchester Art Treasures Exhibition, inviting photographers to contribute their best work. Here was Rejlander's opportunity. His imagination caught fire, and by its light he must have visualised a vast photographic allegory, alive with splendid nudes and graceful creatures in flowing classical robes.

Soon the cartoon took shape which gave the key to the composition, and parts were allocated to members of his 'stock company'. But the most prominent rôles were not for them, and he sought professional models elsewhere.

Rejlander's attempts at photographic idealism soon ran into difficulties. There were 'the stiff-limbed models, who could not assume expressive attitudes, but suffered their limbs to be moved like those of so many lay-figures; the female models, who were far too conscious of their semi-nudity to conceal their feelings; and the grinning models, who would insist upon regarding the whole affair as a gigantic joke.'[37] This may explain why Rejlander obtained some professional models.

Witness to the artist's struggle was Sir Coutts Lindsay, a young and wealthy connoisseur and aristocrat, who had studied art in Rome, where he may first have become acquainted with the Swede. Whatever the circumstances, Rejlander appears to have enjoyed his patronage throughout his life.

The photographic studies were begun early in March 1857, and by the deadline in April at least two complete prints of *The Two Ways of Life* were ready. The Prince Consort was informed, and the following note appeared in the Wolverhampton press:

'Mr O. G. Rejlander, of this town, had the honour of an interview with Prince Albert, at Buckingham Palace, on Tuesday, when he submitted to the inspection of His Royal Highness, a large and well-executed photograph exhibiting a combination of sixteen figures which he has recently succeeded in producing for the forthcoming exhibition in Manchester.'[38] (Note: 'sixteen figures' should, in fact, read 'sixteen groups and figures'.)

Albert, like the Queen, had practical knowledge of collodion photography, and took a lively interest in the affairs of the Photographic Society of London. He had also formed a unique collection of photographs by the foremost European photographers, and Rejlander's summons to the Palace suggests that he intended to add this remarkable picture to it.

During the interview the Prince demonstrated for Rejlander's benefit a paste for glazing albumen prints, though he regretted he could not divulge its constituents.[39] This may have been 'Clausel's Paste', a compound of Ceylon elemi, oil of lavender, and oil of cloves, which was advertised in July with the recommendation, 'used with much success by Rejlander and other eminent photographers'.[40]

A few days later the *Athenaeum* gave a fuller description: 'his last production, an allegorical representation of "Life" is in many parts masterly —worthy to be painted as a fresco. In the centre of the scene a venerable personage leads two youths through an open gate into the world of Manhood, when, one one side voluptuous Beauty beckons into the pleasure paths, which leads away to Licentiousness, Prostration (sic), Insanity, and Death . . .'

'Altogether, as Mr Rejlander means it to be, the composition is for the artist to study, late and early. Some of the details are ill-chosen; the beings of photography are *all clay*, and the sun brings out their imperfections.'[41]

There was an unexpected preview at the

Birmingham Photographic Society's meeting in Odd Fellows Hall, Temple Street, when, at the close at the meeting Rejlander caused a sensation when he uncovered his great photograph before the members. 'This magnificent picture,' ran the report, 'decidedly the finest Photograph of its class ever produced, is intended to show of how much photography is capable, and how it may be made to assist the artist in historical and other paintings.' This reporter admired particularly the 'splendid figure symbolizing Repentance', and considered it 'worthy of careful observation from every artist'.[42]

The Manchester Art Treasures Exhibition was opened by the Queen on 30 June 1857. Situated in a gigantic mausoleum of brick and glass in Trafford Park, it contained the most valuable collection of pictures and objets d'art ever to be brought together north of the Trent; for in those days Manchester spelt culture as well as cotton. The nobility had lent generously from their ancestral halls, and the walls were covered with Raphaels, Titians, Rembrandts, and Van Dycks; the floors with armour and antique statuary. The photographic display—nearly six hundred pictures assembled by Philip Delamotte, and representing work by the best English and Continental operators—was hidden at the top of a flight of stairs off the water-colour gallery.

The Prince Consort, as patron, exhibited the best of his photographic collection. Described as 'mostly foreign, and very large', these depicted wild mountain scenery and glaciers, the ruins of ancient Rome, and still-life studies of game by Lake Price—thus revealing the explorer, the scholar, and the hunter. There were also photographic copies of drawings by Raphael from the Royal Collection, for this earnest and far-sighted Prince was amongst the first to appreciate the value of photography for the reproduction of the old masters.

Portraits abounded, scarcely one of which showed any trace of the silver image beneath its coating of oil paint;[43] a hybrid style justified by the shortcomings of the wet-plate. There were also some fine architectural photographs, as well as Dr Diamond's pictures of insane women.

Rejlander's contribution was *Children* (probably *After Raphael's Sistine Madonna*); '*What Ails Amy?*', a composition print; and *The Two Ways of Life*, below which hung a small inscription in Rejlander's black letter, dedicating the picture to British artists. This photographic sampler was intended to 'sell' photography to figure artists, but unfortunately Rejlander's guileless intention was overlooked by the critics, who judged it either according to the canons of classical art, or upon moral grounds.

Remarking that allegorical subjects 'are rather beyond the capabilities of photography', one critic added that 'we cannot keep back a meed of praise from the works of Baldus, Lake Price, and Rejlander. This latter gentleman will readily understand why we prefer his earlier works, such as "*Don't Cry, Mamma*", *Barnaby Happy*, and *The Scholar's Mate*, etc, to those he now exhibits. The best of these is that of the cherubs from the picture of the *Madonna del Siste*; this is done from the life, though the angels are rather too much "of the earth, earthy". . . A more ambitious picture is that of "*Youth and Age*" (*The Two Ways of Life*), exhibiting extraordinary ingenuity and skill, being printed from some thirty negatives; the picture has many good points, but falls somewhat short of our idea of allegory, as delineated, ought to be.'[44]

No doubt Victoria examined the picture closely while Albert explained the allegory. It is unlikely that Her Majesty would have been repelled by its display of semi-nudity, for, except to the Nonconformist mind there was less objection to nudity in art at that time than was the case later in the century. It is said that Albert's copy was purchased for him by the Queen.[45] Years later it was stated that it had hung in the Prince's suite at Windsor Castle; though a newspaper item

TWO WAYS OF LIFE, OR HOPE IN REPENTANCE, exhibiting at Manchester, 31×16, £10. 10s. 0d. Original Studies of do., 5s. and 7s. 6d. Reduced Copy of ditto, 16×8½, 12s. 6d. Ariadne, 10s. 6d.; ditto, Stereoscopic, 2s. 6d. Photographed from Life, by O. G. Rejlander, Esq.

The above, and all the beautiful Photographs of this eminent Artist, can be had wholesale and retail, of the publishers,—

BECKINGHAM & CO.,
PHOTOGRAPHIC CHEMISTS,
103, GREAT HAMPTON ST. BIRMINGHAM.

AGENTS FOR OSBORNE'S DEVELOPING BOX AND SUTTON'S PHOTOGRAPHS.

Fig 3 The Two Ways of Life, *or* Hope in Repentance. *Beckingham's advertisement in* Photographic Notes, *1857*

published two years after the Prince's death stated that it had hung in his dressing-room at Balmoral;[46] but it has since disappeared.

In April 1858 Rejlander addressed the Photographic Society of London on the subject of *The Two Ways of Life*, and in his peculiar and circumlocutary fashion explained his motives, revealed his technique, and unravelled the allegory.[47]

The composition was to be competitive with what might be expected from abroad; it was to show artists how this technique would enable them 'to judge of effect before proceeding to the elaboration of the finished work'; and it was to demonstrate the 'plasticity of photography', which explains why he brought in figures draped and in the nude, 'some clear and rounded in the light, others transparent in the shade'. In justification of photography he added: 'I *cannot* understand how a painting upon the same subject can, except in its colouring, be more real or truthful than a photograph, both being but representative.'

He revealed that the picture was executed in six weeks, 'with a small Ross's lens, and patched cracked camera, and a pressure-frame (printing-frame) not half the size of the picture—employing a model now and then, draped in a bit of unbleached calico'.

His method of printing was, however, contrary to the art of drawing. 'I began with the foreground figures,' he explained, 'and finished with those farther off. After having fixed upon the size of most of the nearest figures, I proceeded with those in the second plane. With a pair of compasses I measured on the focussing glass the proportionate size according to the sketch; similarly with the third plane, and so on until I was as far off the smallest group as my operating-room would allow, and then I was not far enough off by yards: so I reversed the whole scene and took them from a looking-glass, thus increasing the distance.'

The picture was too large for a single sheet of printing paper, so 'The papers were chosen from the same maker, and sensitised at the same time, to ensure the same tint after having been in the hypo; but even then it happened that the two sheets turned with a different tint...'

Having printed in all the figures he looked around for a suitable background; 'in the place where I reside there is not within some considerable distance any sign of classical architecture. So I went into a friend's grounds and selected from his garden ornaments and portico what you see, excepting the draperies, which were arranged in my room, which is not 12 feet high.'[48]

Describing the allegory, he went on: 'In the background is represented a country scene, where, far from the tumult of life, two youths have been fondly reared. The time has arrived when duty calls them to perform their part in the busy haunts of men. The father, with many misgivings, but with many prayers, conducts them from the home of their childhood, through an archway, which is symbolic of the boundary between town and country. Left orphans at an early age, the spirit of the mother is seen still hovering near them, instilling into their minds good desires, and attending them as a guardian angel...'

'The Sage counsels them: "My sons, if sinners entice thee, consent thou not: Keep thy father's commandment, and forsake not the law of thy mother: That they may keep thee from the strange woman, from the stranger that flattereth with her words..."'

'With faith in his leader and guide, one of the youths appears willing to be led by wisdom and experience, and is thus brought into the paths which lead to *Religion.*—Near to Religion is *Knowledge*—the book being a sign of human progress. From these we come to *Mercy*, who binds up the wounds of the sufferer. The proper use of life is further illustrated by *Industry, Handicraft*, and *Mental Application*; whilst *Married Life* is faintly traced behind the group of *Industry.*'

'The other youth, more impulsive, braves the future for the present: believing in nought but what he sees, he slips the hand of his guiding friend, and, strong in his own conceit, goes *his* way, the wise man waving his hand in grief. Two *Sirens* with song and dance display their charms to tempt the youth; 'tis but a step;— but in the foreground lies an *Idle* group; Idleness the root of all evil. The *Old Hag* thereby contrasts them well: like them she was; as she, they'll be—. A *Bacchante* is in the foreground placed with the *cup* in either hand: in the deepest shades of that dark Bacchante lurks *Murder* with ready arm. Hid from his view the *Gamblers* play; one wins the throw, foul or fair; the other seems aggrieved, yet ready to drown his anger in the tankard; the third has lost his all, and seems as lost himself. *Complicity* whispers close behind, and some strong arm is drawing off a pinioned man. To the central figure with half-covered head, I have given the name of *Penitence*. She is placed, I think rightly, between the two ways of good and evil, to convey what is taught to and believed by us all, that repentance, if true, will not be refused by *Religion.*'

During the discussion which followed, a member remarked, 'The picture itself has been severely criticised, and it certainly is to be regretted that two or three figures in it, though perhaps not exactly indelicate, verge so closely upon it, as to prevent the *general* approval of the picture'; whereupon Mr Shadbolt jumped to Rejlander's defence. 'I most strongly dissent from the opinion expressed by Mr Crace, that there is *any* portion of it which is offensive to delicacy.'

Rejlander explained, 'If some people have thought any part of that picture at all approaching indelicate (sic), that I cannot help; I never intended it. Perhaps some of the peculiar positions were owing to my wish not to show too great an approach to the Pre-Raphaelites'; meaning, perhaps, that he did not wish to over-emphasise detail.

Another member remarked, 'I have seen Mr Rejlander down at Wolverhampton. He has a very small operating-room in a mining district, in such a very bad town to obtain subjects (models) that I do not know how he managed it. If you were to get up a picture in London, you would, perhaps, procure them readily; but Wolverhampton is the most unlikely place in the world for such a purpose.' But upon this subject Rejlander maintained a tactful silence.[49]

There are four main groups in *The Two Ways of Life*: the *Sirens*, the *Bacchante*, *Penitence*, and the three figures which represent *Religion*, a *Penitent*, and *Knowledge*; the rest are subsidiary. The nude figures are most probably professional models, and there are only two of these.

The *Idle Group* (so called) bears some resemblance to Etty's *Sleeping Nymph and Satyrs*, though without its seductive grace. The tambourine (a symbol of dalliance until its take-over by the Salvation Army) is common to both pictures.

The *Sirens* are well posed, but it is a pity that the youth whom they would beguile, though pleasant, is as stiff as a dummy. Likewise, his righteous brother is no actor.

The *Sage* has an air of intellectual power and authority, but his beard is palpably false. Without it, he appears in a small circle picture dated 22 March 1857.

The *Hag*—the end-product of prostitution—'despised and vengeful', appears frequently in Rejlander's tableaux, and is evidently a woman of character.

At the far right, small enough to be overlooked, is the pleasant little group representing *Married Life*. The characters were posed close to the camera, which was focussed on their image in a mirror on the far wall. The large infant partakes of nature's bounty.

The profile of the student with the globe may not belong to its body, this being one of the facilities of composition photography! The victim in the *Mercy* group wears a head bandage, the time-honoured device in painting and the movies to represent physical injury.

In the original print *Industry* and *Handicraft* wore classical medieval garb, but Rejlander rightly brought them up-to-date in the later version. Of the carpenter with the jack-plane and the mechanic wielding a hammer, the latter is the more plausible. The woman in the background holds a sort of bobbin. This group and its background could not have been taken in the Darlington Street studio. The shadow cast by the pilaster above, and the shadow of the woman's arm show that this is one picture. It may have been taken in the School of Art, nearby.

The groups behind the *Sirens* hold together less well, and are the least convincing. *Complicity* may be a pair of lesbians, and the *Pinioned Man* properly gives the impression of hasty departure.

A defect in the earlier version is the pose of the *Sage*, who appears to be addressing the righteous counterpart instead of showing abhorrence of the dissolute groups. The Fifth Commandment was inscribed on the pedestal on the right, but this was deleted in the later version when the *Religion-Penitence-Knowledge* group was moved slightly to the left, improving the general effect. The join between the two sheets of sensitised paper originally struck vertically down along the left-hand edge of the pillar, cutting *Religion's* veil; but in the Royal Photographic Society original the join is less obvious, being carried around the edge of the veil, following the drape which flows from the head of *Penitence*.

Complicity was later moved to the corner behind the vine-wreathed pillar. One wonders, incidentally, where did Rejlander obtain vine leaves in early spring? *Murder*, hiding behind a jardinière was less happily re-sited between the *Sage* and *Penitence*.

Rejlander must have made at least five separate printings of *The Two Ways of Life*. There was the Manchester copy, which may have been that purchased by the Queen; and the copy shown to the Birmingham Photographic Society was another. The Scottish physicist, Sir David Brewster, obtained a copy for 10 guineas in 1858;[50] and a copy believed to have been sold by Rejlander in 1870 was presented to the Royal Photographic Society in 1925. This may be the only original in existence. Also in that year, J. Dudley Johnston, president of the society, stated, 'a few years ago a gentleman from Streatham called on me and told me he possessed a copy bought by his grandmother from Rejlander about sixty-five years ago'.[51] This may, of course, have been a smaller copy.

Various influences may be identified in *The Two Ways of Life*. There are similarities of arrangement and background with Raphael's *The School of Athens*, and Couture's *Les Romains de la Décadence*, the latter a languid

21

orgy in wide-screen romanesque.[52] But there is more than a hint that Rejlander had read *The Mysteries of London* (1846), by George Reynolds, for in its prologue is written:

'From this city of strange contrasts branch off two roads, leading to two points totally distinct the one from the other.'

'One winds its tortuous way through all the noisome dens of crime, chicanery, dissipation, and voluptuousness; the other meanders amidst rugged rocks and wearisome acclivities, it is true, but on the wayside are the resting-places of rectitude and virtue.'

'Along those roads two youths are journeying.'

'They have started from the same point; but one pursues the former path, and the other the latter.'

One of Rejlander's kinder critics remarked that the picture reminded him of the *poses plastiques* affairs arranged at certain questionable places of entertainment. This opinion was confirmed years later when the artist informed John Werge that he had had the services of 'Madame Wharton's *poses plastiques* troupe' when he was making the studies for the composition.[53]

In these displays, which flourished during the mid-Victorian period, male and female models clad in fleshings enacted tableaux representing famous paintings and sculptures; the bill sometimes being shared with a nigger minstrel band. Renton Nicholson, gossip, versifier, and connoisseur of London night-life, produced such performances in conjunction with the notorious 'Judge and Jury Society', which rather tainted this image of art for art's sake.[54]

One of these shapely performers was Eliza Crowe, who had married a male model named Warton. She had posed for William Etty,[55] famous for his nudes, and Ford Maddox Brown, the Pre-Raphaelite painter.[56] Her independent career began in October 1847 at Sutton House, Leicester Square, where she personated Venus, Ariadne, Junveen, Sappho, and Diana. In the following year she enacted Lady Godiva's famous ride in that equestrienne's home town, Coventry. Her husband, personating the Black Prince, rode less comfortably, encased in a suit of armour.

But Rejlander's memory may have been at fault, for there is no record of Madame Warton's troupe performing in or near Wolverhampton in the spring of 1857, the period when the studies were being taken for *The Two Ways of Life*. Fifty years later, a writer quoting hearsay suggested the models came from Manchester,[57] but there is no evidence that she was performing there either.

There is a footnote to the mystery. In February 1858, less than a year after the great composition was completed, Wolverhampton was plastered with large yellow playbills advertising Madame Laurant's *poses plastiques*, that lady 'having the honour of appearing every evening in Eleven Single Figures—Lady Godiva, Sappho, Ariadne, etc etc'. Beneath a cut depicting Madame Laurant strumming a lyre from the top of a large boulder, there is this legend:

'The Provincial Press had, in all cases, given the most unqualified and eulogistic report of Madame Laurant's Company, which in point of arrangement and gorgeousness of accessories far surpass even the once deservedly popular Madame Warton's.'[58] This suggests that she may have belonged to Madame Warton's troupe, and that it had been disbanded. Could Madame Laurant, therefore have been one of the two professional models who posed in the semi-nude for Rejlander's opus?

Following the Art Treasures Exhibition, *The Two Ways of Life* went on show at the South Kensington Museum. 'The pose of each figure is good,' wrote a critic, 'and the grouping of the whole is as nearly perfect as possible. We do not, however, desire to see many advances in this direction. Works of High Art are not to be executed by a mechanical contrivance. The hand of man, guided by the heaven-born mind, can alone achieve greatness in this direction.'[59]

Another writer commented, 'The *quasi* sentimentalism about the indelicacy of the picture, we have no patience to discuss; it would seem that anything which bears with it the impress of antiquity, however lewd or indelicate, is idealized into classicism, whilst anything like an attempt to elucidate an idea in the present *moral* age, if only bordering on the nude, is at once condemned as indelicate. But to the consideration of this class of art, we think that those photographers who are capable of producing such ingenious and clever things by the camera—those who have such a power of composition, are mistaken in their vocation . . .'[60]

Late in 1857 the picture was exhibited at the Scottish Photographic Society's exhibition in Edinburgh, and shortly the following clip appeared in Thomas Sutton's *Photographic Notes*:

'We hear with some surprise that the Scottish Photographic Society have refused to admit *The Two Ways of Life*, a subject intended to teach a high moral lesson, which is certainly the cleverest photograph that has yet been produced. We sincerely hope no such prudery will find its way south of the Tweed.'[61]

Rejlander soon learned that the exclusion was not upon aesthetic grounds, and that certain accusations had been levelled against him.[62] He was perplexed, for did not the picture point a moral?

The picture, probably Brewster's copy, was exhibited in Edinburgh the next year, the dissolute half being curtained off. A contemporary observer remarked that 'in the most prominent place of all in the Exhibition [stands] an entirely *nude* Venus de Medici, by Allinari (does being Italian make a difference?), nude from top to toe!'[63]

Perhaps to make amends, Rejlander had contributed *The Scripture Reader*, a composition which was incapable of offending anyone's susceptibilities.

In 1858 Rejlander met a photographer from Leamington named Henry Peach Robinson, who quickly picked up the composition technique and improved upon it. In that year Robinson exhibited *Fading Away*, a composition from five negatives which aroused almost as much outcry as *The Two Ways of Life*, though for a different reason. It depicted a young girl supposedly dying of consumption; a subject rather too close to reality.[64] Robinson took the hint, and although he exhibited compositions for many years, some of unsurpassed technical excellence, his subjects were often bloodless and artificial.

Rejlander's photographs were exhibited in the chief continental cities. In the United States his work appears to have been first seen in 1862, when Professor Edwin Emerson of Troy University showed *The Two Ways of Life* and several other compositions to the American Photographic Society in Boston. It was reported that 'composition prints are so great a novelty that these pictures justly received marked attention'.[65]

His pictures were now looked for at exhibitions, and he stood his meed of criticism. 'What I complain of,' wrote a scribe, of the Dublin Exhibition, 'is that his last productions should have been more objectionable than that to which I have alluded [*The Two Ways of Life*]—In one of the inner rooms there hangs a frame in one corner of which is represented or attempted to be represented, a man in the seventh stage of life; and in the opposite corner, a hideous object, which I first took to be a representation of the gorilla—and a more revolting object in the form of human being I never saw; but in the centre of the frame Mr Rejlander has taken care to give the eye of the spectator some relief by a photograph of the beautifully formed figure of his model, artfully posed, so as to *focus* the attention of the spectator . . .'[66]

Not insensitive to criticism, Rejlander wrote to Robinson, 'I am tired of photography for the public—particularly composite photos, for there

23

can be no gain and there is no honour, but cavil and misrepresentation. The next exhibition must then only contain ivied ruins and landscapes for ever—beside portraits—and then stop.'[67]

The controversy over *The Two Ways of Life* would have died a natural death had not the uncompromising Thomas Sutton been invited, in January 1863, to address the Photographic Society of Scotland in Edinburgh. It should be recalled that Rejlander had presented him with a copy of the picture in August 1857, for which Sutton had thanked him fulsomely in the columns of *Photographic Notes*. However, times had changed, and now he inveighed against art (or composition) photography, invoking theology to reinforce his argument. '... man is also the noblest creation of the Deity, and if you follow up this train of thought, you will see that pictures which are the result of human imagination, observation, and *powers of imagination*, are more noble than, and belong to a different class—than the images in a camera obscura ... The true artist who has mastered the mechanical difficulties of his profession, and takes a high view of its intellectual dignity, will never attempt to build up pictures by photography; in fact, to an accomplished artist, the method would be much too slow, troublesome, and ridiculous.'

Continuing in a style whose freedom would be the envy of this libel-conscious age, he added: 'When the Council of this Society, some years ago, banished from the wall of its exhibition a photograph entitled the *Two Ways of Life*, in which degraded females were exhibited in a state of nudity, with all the uncompromising truthfulness of photography, they did quite right, for there was neither art nor decency in such a photograph; and if I expressed a different opinion at the time, I was wrong. There is *no* impropriety in exhibiting such works of art as Etty's *Bathers Surprised by a Swan*,—but there *is* impropriety in publicly exhibiting photographs of nude prostitutes, in flesh and blood truthful-

ness and minuteness of detail.'[68]

Rejlander replied to the attack a month later, from the platform of the South London Photographic Society. First defending composition photography, he said, 'The manual part of photographic composition is but wholesale vignetting', vignetting being both 'allowed and admired'. Then, paraphrasing Sutton, he remarked, 'But as there is no mind in the photographic picture, so according to some it cannot contain any new idea, pose, light, or expression capable of representing impressions produced on the human mind, and "not being a work of man" it must be, indirectly, the work of the devil—and, since as "the work of man is indirectly the work of God", as Mr Sutton has it, where are we to go to?'

Defending the reputation of his models, he said: 'There are many female models whose good name is as dear to them as to any other woman. But I prefer to believe that Mr Sutton did not use these harsh expressions on mere supposition; but that he may have been misinformed in his search for truth, by those who wished to increase their attraction by saying that they had been models for Mr So and So; for I have been told that it is not an uncommon practice.'

Sutton did apologise, but had the last word: 'at the same time we have no morbid sympathy for Traviatas and Fleurs de Marie, and do not desire to see such unfortunates figuring in a state of nature in composition photographs upon the walls of a public Exhibition room.'[69]

Concerning art critics, Rejlander related an unfortunate experience which has its present counterpart in the realm of theatre. In a topical photographic allegory entitled *A Vision from Aspromonte,* wherein, garbed as the fallen hero Garibaldi he had lain on the studio floor, pointing dejectedly towards 'Rome', supported by a draped female figure representing 'Hope'. The *Athenaeum* called it indecent, and implied unkindly that 'Garibaldi' had earned a mere fifteen pence for posing. Rejlander revealed that he had been his own model, declaring that he had not realised even sixpence per hour since the critic had 'killed' the picture, issued as a carte-de-visite.[70]

Rejlander's Wolverhampton period is characterised by his genre and tableaux, inspiration for these being derived from his surroundings. *The Washing Day*, for example, is a studio reconstruction of a weekly occurrence beneath his own studio window, impossible to photograph *in situ* on account of the steam. The amnesic old gentleman in '*I have lost my pen, and now my spectacles are gone*'[71] is the Rev George Cottam, who issued the town's marriage licences. Perhaps Rejlander had seen him in just such a state. Mary Rejlander, amused, peeps round the door. The picture also reveals the roof slope and skylight of the studio.

'*Take care of your complexion*' came from the streets: 'Seeing some children at play, mimicking some fair dames they had recently seen stepping mincingly along, holding up as parasols some rag-decorated sticks (actually sticks of rhubarb), and lisping affectedly the words quoted above, Rejlander stopped to amuse himself by observing them. One little fellow, being unable to secure a parasol for himself, cried, "I'll hide my face", and at once buried it in the skirts of another's dress. Here was the suggestion.' There was no question of carrying the heavy camera with its impedimentia down to the street, so the scene was re-enacted in the studio.[72]

Drunken Barnaby Leaving the Tavern may have been inspired by Etty's picture of the same title,[73] though the photograph probably depicted the same smocked character as in *Barnaby Happy* and '*I Pays!*'

'*Don't Cry, Mama*' would appear to have undertones of the recent war in the Crimea.

Rejlander's probable debt to *The Mysteries of London* has already been noted; but it is more than coincidence that later in the book one comes across *The Old Hag*—the key figure to the dissolute half of *The Two Ways of Life*. And there are remarks and exclamations in italics which—verbatim, or in the paraphrase—appear to have inspired several photographs: '*Don't cry, Mummy*' ('*Don't Cry, Mamma*'); '*Second edition!*'; *Found drowned*; and '*I never saw you look so well as you appear this evening*' ('*You look as well as ever you did*'). *The Toilette* may have been suggested by the following passage:

'Lady Cecilia was seated near her toilette-table, with a little gilt-edged oval-shaped mirror in her hands, which reposed on her lap; and Sarah was engaged in arranging the really beautiful hair of her mistress.'

The story involves its hero in the political turmoil of Italy; which, by coincidence, parallels Rejlander's own reputed campaigning with Garibaldi.

Rejlander may never have been convinced that photography was not the medium for allegory. Probably he felt that its way of accentuating the unessential could be overcome by judicious 'sun printing' to darken the offending areas. But allegory came to him quite naturally, and *Infant Photography* is an expression of his feeling for the new art. '. . . infant art—is represented by a dimpled little cupid, gracefully posed beside a camera, upon the lens of which is placed one of his plump little hands, while the other stretches forth a new brush about to be received by a hand bearing a palette, the fellow of which proffers the golden fee'.[74]

The Young Oak in the Old Oak's Arms, a rather far-fetched allegory, shows Rejlander's facility for catching the popular mood during the militia recruitment campaign of the early sixties.

Rejlander argued that 'There is among artists a conventualism that when a man is drawn of great muscle, for the sake of keeping, all the muscles in the body are drawn apparently equally developed, which could scarcely happen', and that 'of those muscles which are greatly excited, the opposite ones are just as quiescent'.[75] The wrestling studies were taken to prove this point. A critic pointed out, however, that 'conventionality has made a law, and now it would seem to be as irreversible as that of the Medes and Persians'.[76]

Even Darwin, noting that the grief muscles in the Laocoön were carried in transverse furrows across the whole breadth of the forehead—'a great anatomical mistake', forgave it 'for the sake of beauty'.[77]

During the summer of 1860 Rejlander visited London, where he was interviewed by that indefatigable columnist in art and photography, Alfred Henry Wall: 'Behold us, four in number,' he wrote, 'sitting in the coffee-room of the — Hotel, before a table covered with the beautiful photographs of Rejlander, just tumbled out of their portfolios. Rejlander, with his fine *os frontis*, keen bright blue-grey eyes, and bearded chin: full of pantomimic action and genial cheerfulness, gives us information of value whenever he speaks, either to the editor of this Journal, or myself . . .'

'We are talking about Rejlander's more recent production, *The Disciple*. The stranger asks "Who was the original painter?" The Editor wonders, "Where on earth he got his model from", and I am drinking in huge gulps of enthusiasm and admiration.'

'Rejlander says, "Much may be done with even the worst model", bending the joints of an imaginary doll into an expressive attitude. "Remember how much expression you may get out of your lay figure if you know how to go about it." '

They examine *The Head of John the Baptist in a Charger*. 'For two long years did that head walk about on a living body, in the eyes of one yearning for its decapitation. At length the opportunity came, the deed was done, he took it off, and there, on a napkin in the charger, it is before

us—"I always saw that head as you see it now," said Rejlander; "that model never came before me without having his head in a charger." '

' "Look here," he cries, "I have created a new goddess, the goddess Nicotina; it is a moral lesson, take a copy and show it to all smokers." "Do you smoke?" asks the stranger of the moral-preaching photographer. Rejlander makes a comically wry face, which he affects to conceal, and replies, "Yes, I do!" '

He shows *Charity*, *The Wrestlers*, a photograph of himself in the quiet enjoyment of a cigar, *Photography receiving a fee from the Painter*, other allegories entitled *Slaves Made Tyrants*, and *The Young Oak within the Old Oak's Arms*, each of which is greatly admired.

He points to a picture of a blind woman: 'I saw her in the street,' he said. 'She was singing " *'Tis dark without, 'tis light within*"; and attracted by the words of her song, I stopped, and, suddenly, it flashed upon me—there *was* light within. I got her to sing to me in my glass-room; when the expression I was so eager to secure came, I said, sing lower, now hum it (all of which Rejlander does), then off came the cap of my lens, and I said, exultingly, "I've got it!" '

The interview terminated upon the inevitable subject of *The Two Ways of Life*. As a purely tentative experiment, Rejlander regretted it had not been received more encouragingly, for then he would have executed others far surpassing it. It was bitter fruit when after expending so much labour, thought, and time, the production turned out to be such as neither did any good to others nor rewarded him.[78]

It may have been during this visit to London that Rejlander was inspired to take one of his most popular photographs, one which was copied and reproduced many times long after he was dead and forgotten. At that period London swarmed with homeless children, sent out to beg and steal in order to survive.[79] As Rejlander was passing at night through one of the mean streets

Our appeal hasn't changed in 125 years . .

Neglected and unwanted children still need your help!

near the Haymarket, he came across a poor child asleep in a doorway, whose crouched attitude seemed to express dejection and hopelessness rather than slumber. On his return to Wolverhampton he procured a similar—and probably cleaner—urchin, dressed him in suitable rags, and posed him in a similar manner in the studio. The study was first exhibited in 1861, when it immediately attracted notice and comment. Combining reality with sentiment, it not only told a story but pointed to a social problem which was literally on the doorstep. Known under various titles, probably *Poor Jo* was the most popular, after the crossing-sweeper in *Bleak House*.

The same urchin appears in three other studies, each posed in the studio. *Tickle-tickle* shows him scratching his foot. In *Day in Town* —a complimentary picture to *Poor Jo*—he is doing a hand-stand. On the wall is chalked '6 times for halfpenny', and on the plank door,

'O.G.R.'. A small girl watches listlessly as the boy tosses stones in a game of 'five-stones', the boy's glance above the top of the picture creating an illusion of movement; the same trick is used in *The Juggler*.

At this period the calotype and the elegant daguerreotype, now almost things of the past, were exchanged for the wet-plate, admittedly a Pandora's box of trouble, but more sensitive, allowing enlargement and indefinite reproduction. Rejlander was not alone in coping with its bugbears, which affected the success of his pictures, and therefore of his livelihood. He had no soundly based knowledge of photographic chemistry, so that many of these troubles must have mystified him, both as to their cause and to their eventual disappearance. On this subject he addressed the Birmingham Photographic Society in 1860 on *The Camera of Horrors; or Failures in the Wet-Plate*.[80]

One of his problems was to discover what caused the cracking of the varnish used to coat the negatives when dry. Mysteriously, this had affected a quarter of the plates he had exposed in 1861, including a portrait he had taken of the Prince Consort.

Albert died of typhus in December 1861 at the early age of forty-two. Unjustly criticised during his lifetime, the English made amends by purchasing his carte-de-visite portrait in vast quantities. Many of these were pirated copies, as Rejlander found to his cost.

The Prince was the first patron of photography in England, and his loss was keenly felt. We do not know to what extent Rejlander's career had been promoted by his patronage, but it was hinted that things were never the same thereafter for the Swedish artist. However, Rejlander's resolve not to make another composition picture was set aside in his desire to commemorate his patron, but there is no evidence that it ever materialised.

The Volunteer Movement sprang into being in

1860 in a popular reaction to the possibility of invasion from France, Louis Napoleon's intentions towards this country being uncertain. An unpaid militia, its members were attracted mainly from the middle and professional classes; and the antics of the small tradesman learning the arts of war were an inspiration to *Punch* artists. Rejlander, the son of an Army officer, no doubt admired the pursuit of arms, and joined the 1st Wolverhampton Volunteer Company (5th Corps).[81] An excellent marksman, he probably found the camaraderie and healthy exertion were an antidote to the fumes and frustrations of photography.

Run-of-the-mill portraiture could never have appealed to him. His preference was for taking art studies, which meant that his main professional connections were with artists and agencies in London. By now the demand may have become more selective and sophisticated, and suit-able models would certainly have been easier to acquire in the Metropolis. There would be an advantage in setting up a studio near, say, St John's Wood, the home of many well-known painters and illustrators. So on 9 April 1862, the following advertisement in the *Chronicle* closed what Rejlander described as the 'better', or happier, part of his life:

MR. O. G. REJLANDER

RESPECTFULLY informs the Ladies and Gentlemen whose PHOTOGRAPHIC PORTRAITS he has taken, that they may have the "NEGATIVES" at a small price, and also remaining copies on hand at a reduced price, if applied for during the next fortnight, as he is leaving this neighbourhood.

Selections from his large collection of ART STUDIES, mounted and unmounted, may also be obtained at very low prices prior to his removal.

Mr. Rejlander takes this opportunity to express his regret at leaving his friends in Wolverhampton, where he has spent the better part of his life, and will be happy to see them again at his Gallery, 5, HAYMARKET, LONDON.

Fig 5 A notice in the Wolverhampton Chronicle, *9 April 1862*

MALDEN ROAD

Rejlander's premises 1862-9, 129 Malden Road, London, NW5, photographed 7 July 1969

No 5 Haymarket was occupied by Joseph Hogarth, printseller and publisher,[1] with whom Rejlander probably had already had business dealings. Next door, John Hogarth Jr carried on a photographic business. Apart from the two great theatres, the street consisted of small shops, oyster bars, cutlers, and tailors; and the surroundings swarmed with Italian and French émigrés. The move may have been temporary while Rejlander looked around for a suitable site on which to build a studio of his own, closer to the ideals of an artist.

Daylight was essential to a photographer's livelihood, and he reasoned that he could not have too much of it. But this theory was not entirely true, for only a limited amount of light actually fell on the sitter relative to that reflected back from all parts of the room. In consequence, negatives were often so flat that they required intensification. In addition, this being a well-clothed period, the glass-room could be turned into a Turkish Bath in hot weather.

Rejlander argued 'that greater solidity and force would be secured if all the light which had no part in the formation of the photographic image—could be either cut off or shut out from the room'; and he experimented first with a tunnel of screens in front of the lens, and later with telescopic tunnels of various shapes and sizes whose interiors were painted dead black.[2]

During the winter and spring of 1862-3 he erected a studio which conformed to his unorthodox theory at the rear of no 7 St George's Terrace, Malden Road, NW. It was 10 x 11ft, and stood near the house, with an entry from a back room down a short flight of stairs. It faced the tunnel, a dark tapering passage 20ft long in which the camera was set up, and at the end of which was a small darkroom.

'It will be seen that the sitter is lighted from the side and top side; front light, and direct vertical light being entirely avoided,' wrote Wharton Simpson. 'The camera is in comparative darkness, enabling the operator to focus without the aid of a dark cloth over his head. The eye of the model also looks into this darkness, by which is gained the double advantage of comfort to the sitter and expansion of the pupil of the eye, giving it more depth and expression.'[3]

It was intended to reproduce as nearly as possible the type of lighting customary in the studios of artists; general portraiture was sub-

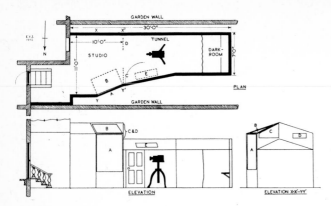

Fig 6 Rejlander's tunnel studio, Malden Road, London, 1863, based upon contemporary diagrams; dimensions are given where known.
A white plate glass window 7 x 5ft
B white plate glass window 5 x 3ft
C, D and E subsidiary windows with blinds.
Studio interior painted white; tunnel black.
Material: corrugated iron on wooden framework.

ordinate. Doubts were expressed as to whether there would be sufficient light on dull days. After two or three weeks' experience Rejlander replied: 'As to light, I have abundance without overflowing, but "just the ticket"—I took a group of twelve last Wednesday, plenty of light for all.'[4]

The merits and demerits of the tunnel studio were argued in the photographic press, and some earnest amateurs even applied to Rejlander himself. Receiving no reply, one complained to *Photographic News*. 'You must not readily come to the conclusion of intentional discourtesy,' admonished Wharton Simpson. 'Letter writing to busy persons is often a bore, and successful artists are very much overwhelmed with such enquiries, and they are sometimes driven, in self defence, to a disregard, which is erroneously attributed to discourtesy.'[5]

Rejlander's reply probably saved him from

further bother: 'It seems rude, but I have a great aversion to letter writing, particularly to writing the same thing over and over again, that, I have done; and when I say I am a bad correspondent, even in cases that concern my own interest, I hope to be forgiven.'[6]

This corrugated-iron structure of uncompromising ugliness made photographic history, for here Rejlander took some of his best studies. Today, the site is a sad scene of desolation—but fascinating, nevertheless, for on 28 March 1863 a diffident young clergyman came here to have his portrait taken. 'Went to Rejlander's (the Photographer),' he entered in his diary, 'and got my picture taken, large and small and half-length. I also looked over a large number of prints and negatives, some of which were very beautiful.'[7] He was Lewis Carroll, and *Alice in Wonderland* was, as yet, unpublished. An admirer of Rejlander's child studies, Carroll later invited the artist to Oxford to advise upon the suitability of Badcock's Yard for his own photographic activities.[8]

The theory of the tunnel studio was sound enough, but it came a little too early in photographic history. Given the faster gelatine dry-plates it would have been ideal; but when this boon arrived, electric light was not far behind.

Each period in history is epitomised by its ideal of female beauty. Rejlander's High-Victorian models express virginal purity. The selection of models depended upon a roving eye; in such manner were the archetype Pre-Raphaelite beauties picked up—Elizabeth Siddall plying her needle in her mother's shop, and Jane Burden in a theatre audience. Rejlander, catching sight of a beautiful girl in the street followed her home. Later, he despatched Mrs Rejlander (excellent woman!) to introduce herself to the young lady, and invite her to give him some sittings. His wife was successful, resulting in some of his finest studies.[9]

The lovely models photographed in the Malden Road studio testify to his extraordinary control over expression and lighting, and to his powerful idealism. *Patience, 'Is It True?', Her Portrait* and *Truly Thankful* are typical examples. The lighting generally falls from the top and left, though reflectors were also used. He ignored the intrusion of properties in the background, preferring to move the camera rather than to disturb an expressive pose.

A. H. Wall, a frequent visitor to the studio, recalled that he was 'genial, friendly, talkative, sympathetic, full of anecdote, sprightly, and amusing—made you feel at home with him, made you as anxious to please him as he was to please you, robbed you of all feeling of restraint and strangeness, occupied so much time with each sitter, especially if he had a "good" one, that the pay he received never fairly remunerated him'.

The sitter had no idea that he or she was being subjected to a series of experiments to discover the best lighting and position, 'they only thought him a little eccentric and particular compared with other photographers'.[10]

But even Rejlander had his difficulties. An eminent medical man came to him, retired into himself and proved an impossible sitter. The sitting was postponed. On the second visit Rejlander focussed the camera and then engaged the doctor upon the subject of an illness from which he suffered, the symptoms of which puzzled him. While the doctor was putting his searching questions, the plate was prepared in the obscurity of the tunnel, and at a sign from the photographer a successful exposure was made.[11]

Alma-Tadema, the popular Anglo-Dutch artist and protegé of Sir Coutts Lindsay, was probably one of Rejlander's clients. Several semi-nude studies are suggestive of that artist's immaculately robed Roman maidens, who spend their days luxuriating on sunlit marble terraces. These statuesque *Classic Studies* express no sentiment,

and may have been posed by the client rather than by the photographer.

In complete contrast, Rejlander brought out a photograph which was popular on account of its implied naughtiness. Observing the expression of a friend listening to a risqué story whispered in his ear, he invited the listener to his studio. 'When the focussed plate was in the camera, and the sitter posed, the photographer suddenly left the camera, and putting his lips to his ear, whispered such a story—as he imagined the original one to have been.' Mrs Rejlander, at a signal, uncapped the lens, and the sitter 'with the irrepressible and unconscious glee of the scandalmonger, ejaculated the two expressive words which gave the resulting picture its title, *"Did She?"* '[12]

Rejlander obtained his effects in the darkroom by a mixture of experience and intuition. George Dawson, editor of the *British Journal of Photography*, was enchanted to watch him develop a 10 x 8in or 11 x 9in plate, 'pouring the developer from the mouth of a champagne bottle with apparent carelessness, but really with curious dexterity and skill'. Even so, Dawson was not the only one to note that at times he could be deplorably careless; he disliked the purely mechanical part of photography, which is remarkable when one recalls *The Two Ways of Life*.

Wall observed that 'Any unusual effect, the result of some chance condition, would start him on a new series of experiments which too frequently landed him in a sea of perplexity—. In this way there was often a terrible waste of time, money, and patience.'

Once, in such a mood, he hit upon the Sabattier effect, the subject being a partly nude female figure.

'Look at that!' he cried to Wall. 'Now, tell me, if you can, how that was got. See how it improves the flesh—it's like a bit of Etty's flesh.'

'Only,' replied Wall, 'Etty did it without the thick black outline. How was that got?'

'By accident at first,' cried the triumphant artist, 'but now I can get it when I please.'

Wall concluded, 'And he firmly believed he could, and said he certainly would; but I don't think he did.'[13]

His methods may have been empirical, yet the following anecdote should be taken with a pinch of salt:

'Calling upon Mr Rejlander, the other day—we were introduced to a new instrument for measuring the actinic power of light. The instrument is neither more nor less than a pretty little white cat, and experiment has demonstrated that the shape and size of the pupils—indicate very accurately the amount of light in the studio.—If the pupils are represented by mere black lines he (Rejlander) gives the shortest exposures: if they approach the elliptical he gives long exposures; but if they are round and large, he puts on the cap of his lens and the hat of his head, saying, "Today there will be no exposures, and I may take a walk!" '[14]

Rejlander bore some resemblance to the popular hero, Garibaldi. Whether he had ever been his 'friend and fellow soldier'[15] has yet to be confirmed. However, he issued photographs of himself garbed as the Liberator of Italy, adopting a stance which may have adapted from personal observation. In view of the rarity of authentic photographs, this carte-de-visite was at least more realistic than many engravings, whose points of agreement were limited to the famous beard and the shirt.

Following a photographic tour of the South of England, during which he experienced all the usual pinholes, foggy and streaky negatives customary to the wet-plate during hot weather, Rejlander wrote to Dawson 'to enlist the service of all the photographic world—how to make a collodion sensitive without the nitrate of silver bath'.[16] A reply was not long delayed, when Sayce and Watson described their 'collodio-bromide of silver' process—a major break-through in photographic chemistry.[17]

Photographic exhibitions no longer attracted the general public as they had done when photography was still a novelty. Many amateurs were now shy of competing with those who held the loftiest position in the art. Rejlander deplored this, and wrote suggesting a broadening of the categories of exhibition so that all tastes should be catered for. In a footnote he added: 'In connection with a question arising out of the exhibited works of Julia Cameron (1864, her first exhibition) and which has been pretty widely discussed, without arguing in favour of woolliness and the effect of imperfect vision, much may be said in favour of the idea of having a representation of flesh without an exaggerated idea of the bark of the skin, such as we have seen in many large photographs by eminent photographers ...'[18]

In the following year, a notice of the Berlin Exhibition gave surprising news:

'That well-known photographic artist, whose products at the Berlin exhibition stimulated the most undivided praise of artists and critics, now leaves photography entirely and returns to his original art, portrait painting ... The relatively minor success of his photographic endeavours is the reason for this step, for which we can only be deeply sorry ... Pieces such as *Did She?*, *Madonna from the Sasso Ferrato*, the *Flycatcher*, *Faith*, and many others will be the models of his art which will form a weighty argument for maintaining the view that photography should be regarded as an art in the highest sense. Some day, a history of art-photography will be written, in which the name of Rejlander will be cited as a star of the first magnitude. Rejlander himself is —according to a personal communication made to us by the Crown Princess on the occasion of the Exhibition—a Swede, and enjoyed the special patronage of the late Prince Albert. The repeated setbacks which his works have suffered, when opposed, at several exhibitions, to the works of Robinson (who, it is true, has superior technique) may be a substantial reason for his new step.'[19]

The withdrawal was only temporary, but there is some mystery as to its actual cause. Wharton Simpson explained that 'He (Robinson) and Rejlander are never really in concurrence, and have only occasionally attended the same exhibition simultaneously. Rejlander has participated unluckily in many exhibitions, and in each case his work suffered through some negligence, which detracted from its real beauty and inner truth.'[20]

There was a world of difference between Rejlander and Robinson. Except for Rejlander's misguided essays into the realms of photographic allegory, his characters rang true. They were not just figures in a landscape, admitting, of course, Robinson's partiality for the rustic and the picturesque.

The carte-de-visite boom was in full swing, the print shops featuring a profuse collection of patricians, prelates, and prize-fighters, and other popular or notorious figures. Many of these photographs were pirated copies; some photographers finding piracy a lucrative sideline. Rejlander had undoubtedly been tempted, but justly delivered a broadside in the *British Journal of Photography* against the practice. 'There is quite enough of *drawbacks* against our art without its votaries wilfully making it a low art—quite enough of uphill-fight to keep it in a respectable position.'[21]

By July 1866 Rejlander was bartering '24 or more of his largest and best studies' for a rolling press,[22] probably for lithography. Money, it would appear, was short.

Wall noted his uneven disposition, though sympathetically. 'Rejlander hardly ever attempted to finish his conceptions photographically,' he wrote. 'They were thrown out, as it were, in the rough for after treatment—But alas! in this, as in many other instances, postponement was fatal —the dreamed-of opportunity never came. His battle of life, however, was not an easy one.

Although he encountered all his constantly appearing and disappearing difficulties with a light, bold, Trojan-like heart, and was altogether a genial native of artistic Bohemia—happy, free, and careless, generous, frank and fearless, so that nothing seemed to daunt him, give him lasting grief, or cause him to despair—yet often enough, I doubt not, he grew weary and disheartened. The efforts required to carry out his conceptions, the patient thinking and careful experiments, and the optical and chemical and technical teasings which complicated his labours, must have made him think his plucky little game of art photography hardly worth the candle of time it burnt away too rapidly. I have often heard him say, "I should do better if I abandoned this artistic idea altogether—it don't pay me; and I am half inclined to think it does as little for the advancement of photography." '[23]

But there were compensations: he was in Edinburgh early in 1866, where he was fêted by the leading members of the Royal Scottish Academy; and a dinner was held in his honour by some prominent photographers. The occasion was the opening of the Photographic Society of Scotland's exhibition, at which Rejlander was an exhibitor for the first time since the rejection of his *magnum opus*. The trip combined business with pleasure, for amongst the pictures was a portrait of Dr John Brown, author of *Rab and his Friends*, together with his favourite mastiff.[24]

The question of focus was revived when Mrs Cameron held her one-man show at Colnaghi's later in the year.[25] Most professionals did not question the principle that a portrait must be sharp, but at the same time any scheme was desirable which softened the 'bark of the skin'. Claudet had suggested a means of accomplishing this by actually moving the lens during exposure. Rejlander scoffed: 'Successfully catching positions and expressions of "living life", instantaniety, seem all opposed to movable focus.'[26]

In *Photography as the Handmaid of Art*, Rejlander offered some practical hints to his fellow artists. A contact transparency of a portrait was put in the window against the sky, the rest of the window being darkened, then with the camera he projected an enlarged image to the requisite size on the canvas upon which he proceeded to sketch. Photography, he said, will thus 'save for you the most precious thing you have, *your time,*—no mean service in these electric-torrent-living times...'[27]

To a certain extent Rejlander was preaching to the converted, for many artists were already using photography, though not necessarily in the form Rejlander was suggesting. W. P. Frith, of course, had reached such a pinnacle in the art world that he would not care who knew that he painted his vast tableaux from specially posed photographs. Dante Gabriel Rossetti, on the other hand, may not have stressed that his ideal woman—*Beata Beatrix*—was painted from one of a series of photographs for which Jane Morris had posed inside a large tent.

At the Royal Academy of 1867 Rejlander exhibited *Oscar*; one wonders if it was a portrait of his own child. The only reference to a family is in Wall's description of 'a back-garden view' which included 'himself and child'.[28]

Rejlander does not appear to have abandoned photography for long, for shortly there appeared a series of studies which caught the raw humour of the street-urchin and the crossing-sweeper. He did not need to look far for his models for there was a home for poor boys at Chalk Farm, only half a mile from the studio. '*Jem, is it a good 'un?*', in which the boy bites a halfpenny to make sure it is genuine, is a typical example. But *A Ragged-School Boy* is straight reportage; the boy's stance, one arm drooped over the ornate chair, is a parody of the conventional masculine pose.

There is a curious photograph dating from this period entitled *Sherry Cobbler*, wherein Rejlander sits at a small table stirring a wine glass with a fork-handle. An arsenic-impregnated fly-paper covers his bald patch. On the wall is the photograph of *Poor Jo*. According to *The Concise Oxford Dictionary*, sherry cobbler is an 'iced drink of wine, sugar, lemon, sucked through a straw (origin unknown; from US)'. But why the fly-paper?

In 1868 Rejlander took a portrait of Gustave Doré, the most prolific and the wealthiest illustrator of his time. The picture was shown at the Photographic Society in November, and there was a rumble of criticism. 'How is it that his (Rejlander's) photographic manipulation is so inferior to his artistic ability?—his printing tones and effects are of the worst description. This is particularly noticeable in the portrait of Gustave Doré.'[29]

By contrast, the *Art Journal* remarked, 'it is the best that up to this time has been produced; and it is not likely that there will ever be a better'.[30] And Doré was delighted with it.

The *Art Journal*, an early critic of art photography now devoted an article to *The Photographs of Rejlander*. 'Late years,' it began, 'have shown that more can be done than we at one time thought possible, and that results are obtainable from lens and camera, which are not merely imitations and copies from still nature, but productions of mind and thoughtful study—. Of Mr Rejlander's pictures (for such we may justly call them) we have no hesitation in saying that they are full of beauty and full of mind.' Nevertheless, the writer warns artists against leaning for assistance upon photographic studies, except, for example, for the folds of drapery.[31]

An artist who leaned upon Rejlander for more than the folds of drapery was the Pre-Raphaelite painter, Edward Burne-Jones. In his canvas *Flamma Vestalis* one recognises the same placid, dreamy profile as in the photograph *Truly Thankful*.

By the late sixties photography had reached a point of technical stability, and the enthusiasm was now spent which characterised photographic societies in the early days. The arguments both for and against combination printing were now largely academic, so great had been the improvement both in optics and chemistry. (But Robinson still turned out one massive work yearly 'to go a-medalling with'.) Mrs Cameron's soft-focus effects were generally admired but seldom imitated. The great innovator was a Frenchman, Adam-Salomon, whose portraits exhibited an unusual roundness and plasticity.

Rejlander continued to exhibit, though in November 1868 it was observed that his studies were 'not very new' (*The Two Ways of Life* had turned up again), 'and were familiar to most of his friends and admirers'.[32] But he had other preoccupation, for in the following March his 'friends and admirers' received the following curious but characteristic circular:[33]

129, Malden-road, London, N.W., March, 1869

After 9th April
my photographic studio will
be opened at
No. 1, Albert Mansions,
Victoria-street
opposite Victoria Station, S.W.

I shall need encouragement
and endeavour to deserve it.

O. G. REJLANDER.

ALBERT MANSIONS

84 Albert Mansions, Victoria Street, London, SW1, photographed 15 September 1967. The two arched windows on the right of the SOLAR CLUB *photograph may be identified on the fourth floor*

'Mr Rejlander,' wrote a correspondent to the *Philadelphia Photographer*, 'one of your most skilful and artistic professional photographers, has recently had a new studio built in Victoria Street, Westminster, the center of a very fashionable district. It is not on that account, however, that I refer to the matter, but because the studio is of somewhat unusual and daring construction, and its lighting facilities, though varied, are not

based upon any of the orthodox plans. It is not, in a sense, a glass-house, but rather resembles a handsome sitting-room, with a few magnificent windows, which could be used separately or in conjunction with each other, for lighting the sitter.'[1]

Victoria Street was new, and high, expensive apartment flats were rising on each side. The studio occupied the two top floors of Albert Mansions; a lower floor of the same building was occupied by Arthur Sullivan, who, collaborating for the first time with W. S. Gilbert, was composing *Thespis; or the Gods grown old*. Rejlander had collaborated with the architect in the studio design, and light flooded in from a huge skylight, two large arched windows facing west, and a single window of plate glass, 9 x 7ft, facing north. The latter descending into a groove, allowed access to a flat roof.

It was a considerable investment, and Rejlander probably moved into his new establishment with more faith than capital. One of the first to write about it was Thomas Sutton, who was embarrassingly eulogistic, particularly about the artist himself—'this noble fellow', as he called him![2]

In June, Rejlander invited his friends of the Solar Club to a house-warming, and the group photograph taken during the proceedings shows him in the company of some of the foremost figures in the photographic world.[3] On the left sits William England of the London Stereoscopic Company, whose extensive tours opened up the continent and the United States to the British public. With his back to the camera sits Wharton Simpson, editor of *Photographic News*; and to his right is Jabez Hughes, whose lucrative business in the Isle of Wight enjoyed royal patronage. Leaning back into the window one catches the profile of Walter Woodbury, inventor of the Woodbury type, whose name is perpetuated in *The Oxford Dictionary*. H. P. Robinson sits near Rejlander, who smiles benignly upon the proceedings.

Rejlander's new clients were now the carriage-folk of Pimlico and Belgravia. A typical portrait of this period shows the Hon Mrs Rale posed in the full glory of silk and taffeta. Yet here in 1871 he took one of the finest genre photographs of his career—'*Second Edition!*'—a dramatic study of a newsboy crying the sensational news of Chicago's great fire. This picture suggests the kind of picture he would have taken with a hand camera, had he lived in a later period. It is remarkable that this Rejlander is also the Rejlander of *The Two Ways of Life*.

Artists still dogmatised, with faulty logic, that the camera, a machine, was incapable of being an instrument of the mind. This attitude was further influenced by matters not aesthetic, for their pride was offended by the mechanics and tradesmen who had taken up professional photography, and had adopted the garb and supposed affectations of artists. Also, it was galling to see such characters make fortunes from the sale of cartes-de-visite. There were many reasons why photography did not get a good press, though Rejlander was undoubtedly cheered by the *Art Journal's* acceptance. But he was still ready to hit back when critics scorned his adopted profession. 'We photographers have a good ground of complaint against you art critics,' he wrote, 'for the sneering and overbearing manner in which you assign limits to our powers, and in anything but an encouraging or friendly manner dictate to us what we ought or ought not to do. ... Who disputes that photography is not engraving or lithography, wood engraving or etching? We are satisfied that it is an art in itself, only guided by the general canons of art for successful combination to produce an art-looking result.'[4]

During the celebrated Tichborne trial, a daguerreotype of the real Roger Tichborne was produced to show that his ear was differently formed from that of Orton, the Claimant. In 1870 police photography of malefactors was authorised in England. Both of these factors may have influenced Rejlander to pen an article in the *British Journal of Photography* 'anent the photographing of criminals'—their ears in particular.

'In the profile of the ear is the most certain point of identification, for there is greater diversity in the shape of the ear than in any other part of the head ... I have studied ears for nearly forty years, and although I know several persons with well-shaped ears, I know of only four persons who have *beautiful* ears ... In conclusion, I purpose to make a drawing of fifty different types of human ear, and have it engraved for the British Journal of Photography.'[5] But there is no evidence that he carried out his project.

One wonders whether the French criminologist Bertillon was aware of his views, for some years later he began the classification of ears, as well as noses, chins, and of course, fingerprints.

Rejlander spent his spare time painting portraits in the red-curtained recess overlooking Victoria Street. In 1873 he exhibited a portrait entitled *His First Cup* at the Royal Academy.

In 1871 (or perhaps even earlier) Charles Darwin approached Rejlander in connection with his new work, *On the Expression of the Emotions in Man and Animals*,[6] requiring photographs to illustrate fear, anger, pleasure, surprise, indignation, and so on. In evidence of his histrionic powers, Rejlander himself posed for five of these studies. Taken at various sittings, it would appear that *Disgust* and *Helplessness* were taken later, and in Plate VI, Fig 4 his left shoulder droops as though he had been weakened by illness. His finger-tips are stained, probably with silver nitrate.

Joy is a charming study of a young girl smiling; while *Contempt* shows the expression of a young lady supposedly tearing up the photograph of a despised lover. *Sneering* was represented 'by a lady who sometimes unintentionally displays the canine on one side, and who sometimes can do so voluntarily'—the lady being Mary Rejlander!

Darwin's book was only moderately successful. The first printing was taken up, but the reprint (1873) remained largely unsold during the author's lifetime. If it did not make a fortune for Darwin, indirectly it produced a windfall for the photographer. One illustration, entitled *Mental Distress,* depicted an infant (to the inquisitive, a boy) 'howling his head off'. An enlargement was exhibited, which Baden Pritchard, in his review, called *Ginx's Baby,* after the title of a popular novel.[7] Rejlander objected, but the name stuck, and soon he was inundated with demands for copies. Sixty thousand 24 x 30cm prints and a quarter of a million cartes were produced.[8] It wasn't 'art', but it paid the bills.

Ginx's Baby may have been considered vulgar in the drawing room, and productive of immodest laughter in the servants' hall, but photographically it was a work of some importance, for it had arrested the child's appearance while its body and facial muscles were in vigorous movement, and this was unusual. Referring to the recognised portrayal of the passions, based upon Lebrun, an art critic later affirmed that 'they have been finally scattered to the winds by the wonderful photographs of the late O. G. Rejlander, especially noting the illustrations in Dr Darwin's work on expression, and Ginx's Baby, as examples'.[9]

The Rejlanders appear to have moved from Malden Road after the Albert Mansions studio was opened, and in 1873 they were settled in a small semi-detached villa in Stockwell: 23 East Cottages, later renumbered and renamed 53 Willingdon Road. The modesty of this locality suggests that the Victoria studio may have been a strain on the photographer's resources.

Periodically, the studio appears to have looked after itself while the Swedish art photographer drilled and skirmished with the volunteers. On 7 February 1871, a few days before Louis Napoleon, ex-emperor of the French, joined the beautiful Eugénie in exile on English soil, Volunteer Rejlander, O.G., signed the muster roll of the Artist's Company, 38th Middlesex Rgt;[10] joining such distinguished Academicians as Millais, Leighton, and Richmond.

Rejlander was a champion rifleman, and at an age when men tend to slow down enjoyed the challenge of the field exercises and manoeuvres. There is an amusing picture of him at this period by Rev F. F. Statham who, as president of the South London Photographic Society, was entertaining its members at his home in Clapham. It was a stormy Saturday afternoon, and the dinner was well advanced when Rejlander made his appearance 'clad in his volunteer regimentals, dripping with wet—he looked like a river-god in harness, his face was beaming with happiness and his voice full of cheeriness and hilarity'. His host entreated him to change into some dry clothes, and shortly he reappeared 'dressed in a suit of sable, with tight-fitting double waistcoat reaching to his chin, a coat with a clerically-cut collar, and the well-recognized "choker" peculiar to the "cloth"!' With a face solemn as a judge, he warmed to the occasion, 'and proved himself one of the most facetious and amusing "parsons" '.[11]

In the double-print *O.G.R. the Artist Introduces O.G.R. the Volunteer* he is seen in these two roles. He sent a copy to Robinson, who was waging his own war on behalf of art photography, inscribing it 'O.G.R. introduces himself as a volunteer to H.P.R.', conveying that his help was at Robinson's service.[12]

From about the year 1871, Oscar Rejlander was thought to be suffering from Bright's Disease though it is more probable that it was diabetes. By the early months of 1874 he was a very sick man. A pathetic figure, his clothes hung loosely about him as his body wasted, yet he still attended the studio. But when he became too ill to leave home he watched impotently as his expenses mounted and his capital drained away. Fortunately he had many friends, who assured him that his famous negatives (which he had already mortgaged) would be redeemed, and that a living would be guaranteed to his wife.[13]

Baden Pritchard, on a visit to the small house in Stockwell, recalled that Mary, in an effort to cheer the dying man, suggested that a trip to the seaside would do him good. Dreamily, as if half awake, he said, 'Yes, with Teddy, with Teddy.' She had unwittingly awakened a tragic memory, for on their last visit to the sea they had witnessed a child's death by drowning.

Recollecting the mock battles and hot summer days at the rifle range, the artist-photographer said, 'I shall die a volunteer. Let me be buried as one.' He died at eight in the morning of 18 January 1875.[14] Mary signed his death certificate with a cross, so one may presume that she was illiterate.

Friends from the worlds of art, photography, and journalism were at his graveside at Kensal Green, including Sir Coutts Lindsay,[15] of whose influence on Rejlander much has yet to be discovered. Two volunteers discharged a volley over the casket, military style—an unusual act of homage to a photographer. The unmarked grave is hidden in tall grass amidst a tipsy brotherhood of marble crosses.

Rejlander's affairs were summed up by George Dawson: 'His earlier professional efforts in London—mainly through an error of judgment in respect of locality, partially through his disinclination to work merely for money and pander to the bad taste of ignorant patrons, combined, perhaps with an unwise neglect of care in his mechanical and chemical operations—were not successful; and his after successes, which were undoubtedly great, saddled as they were with very heavy expenses, had barely carried him beyond the pursuit of these early difficulties when the end came.'[16] The error of judgement

may refer to his probable association with Joseph Hogarth in the Haymarket; certainly, in 1862 not a very respectable locality.

At an exhibition of his pictures held in the autumn of 1875 at the Photographic Society there was one new picture—*Happy Days, or Coming from the Fair*. It may have been inspired by some happy incident in the Wolverhampton days, with Oscar and Mary arm in arm, he probably a little less sober than she, and both without a care in the world. To those who had been intimate friends of the Rejlanders it aroused poignant memories.

The next decade was a period of transition in photography. Rejlander had said in 1858 that he 'should be very glad to possess a lens that did not need focussing. I should carry it in my pocket, and with a dry collodion process I should catch positions and expressions in a crowd far better than with my own eyes.' The dry plate had arrived, and although the miniature camera with pentaprism finder was still far in the future, the hand-camera was beginning to make this dream come true. The uses of photography proliferated hand-in-hand with half-tone engraving. Taste was more sophisticated, and Rejlander's once-famous studies were now half-forgotten—though not entirely—for his old friend A. H. Wall ran a series on Rejlander's Art Studies in *Photographic News* during 1886-7.

In December 1889 an exhibition of about 400 of Rejlander's prints was held in London. Dr P. H. Emerson, exponent of the Naturalistic School, wrote it up in bantering terms, damning it with faint praise. He appears to have been ignorant of Rejlander's background and times, and summed him up: 'decidedly no genius, no artist, vain, sentimental, artificial, theatrical, but at the same time tremendously enthusiastic, energetically experimental, and best of all, self-sacrificing'.[17]

Meanwhile, Mary Rejlander had fallen on hard times. One by one she had disposed of paintings and art objects to meet expenses, and finally she parted with the precious negatives themselves. Through the good offices of Snowden Ward, editor of *The Photogram*,[18] who had heard of her plight, she was finally 'installed in a little house near her old home in South Tottenham, and though it is still bare of furniture, she still has her lenses, etc, in possession again'. But the negatives were no longer hers. Today, over four hundred prints, titles, or descriptions of prints attributable to Rejlander have been traced.

A quarter of a century after Rejlander's death an assessment of his contribution to photography was made by Hector Maclean. 'What is noticeable in the prints that have come down to us,' he wrote, 'is the resourcefulness and inventiveness of the mind they indicate. The man seems to have brimmed over with an inexhaustible succession of happy thoughts, which he had not the patience or the ability to paint.' He pointed out that for the last quarter century the advancements in technical details had all been on the side of pictorial negatives.[19]

Rejlander was a genial soul—a clubbable man, full of humour, and an excellent raconteur—aided, no doubt, by his undulating Swedish accent and quaint mannerisms. Wall described him as 'a genial native of artistic Bohemia'. He loved to play chess, and it is interesting that he should describe the composition of *The Two Ways of Life* as though it was a game, 'keeping it day and night in view, like a chess-player playing without the board'.

Wall also remarked that 'although he was not himself a very regular church goer, his religious instincts were always strong, and he was not amongst those who think it a mark of superior intelligence and cleverness to sneer at religion. All nature,' he said, 'was full of arguments demonstrating its supreme importance.'[20]

Of his domestic affairs little is known. Mary must have been indispensable to him on both sides of the camera, but she had no sultry Pre-Raphaelite depths; nor should we have expected it of one engaged in the daily, messy business of collodion photography. Though there may have been some shift of emphasis between the serene idealism of *Summer,* and the gay earthiness of *Happy Days,* one feels that they were a devoted couple. There is no mention of children in the obituary.

Hard Times may have been autobiographical, for Rejlander's affairs appear to have skated upon the edge of solvency. The carpenter's ghostly counterpart undoubtedly portrays a destitute man, and may be the recollection of harsh experience.

There is occasional evidence of a strange, surrealistic imagination in his photographs, something odd. What, for instance, was one to make of *Sherry Cobbler* and its arsenic fly-paper?; the woman biting the blanket, with whose feet upon her shoulders?; the troubled children with the mask?; the ghoulish *Nicotina?*; and *The Dream?*

Recently a medical man, who knew nothing of Rejlander, provided a clue when he was confronted with a random selection of his works. Being asked what they suggested to him of the artist's psyche, he replied, 'Schizophrenia'.

This opinion could explain Rejlander's periods of dynamic creative ability, followed by 'grey' periods of mental torpor, when careless work slipped through—not unnoticed by the critics. It is the production of *The Two Ways of Life,* rather than the product, which makes it one of the curiosities of early photography.

But this picture alone is insufficient to grant Rejlander a permanent place amongst those who have given photography what it has of an artistic form. His real contribution was summed up shortly after his death by a writer who perceived that 'he saw things unconventionally, which is what few photographers do; he did not weary us with insisting on detail where it was not needed, and he gave full opportunity to the happy accidents of nature'.[21]

PHOTOGRAPHIC ART STUDIES
AND PORTRAITS
BY O.G.REJLANDER

1, St GEORGES TERRACE

MALDEN ROAD

HAVERSTOCK HILL

———

ABBREVIATIONS

ABB   Dr A. Beryl Beakbane Collection,
        England
BCS   Bäckström Collection, Stockholm
EPS   Edinburgh Photographic Society
GEH   George Eastman House, Rochester, NY
GCUT   Gernsheim Collection, University of
        Texas
KM   Kodak Museum, Harrow, England
RPS   Royal Photographic Society, London

Reverse of Rejlander's carte-de-visite. Note sunflower and palette motif

THE WASHING DAY c1854-6 GCUT
'... we could not easily forget the "washing scene", with figures hanging up the clothes and others in the suds, which could not be produced without a great amount of genius on his part, and practice in the drilling of the models.' (*Journal of the Photographic Society of London*, 21 April 1858)

LONGING FOR HOME   1855   RPS
'...a sailor boy's face with a broad square forehead and black hair driven over it—just such a lad as would cram shot into a cannon, or nail up the colours amid a hail of shot.' (*Athenaeum*, 1856)

FORTUNE-TELLING 1855 RPS

One of the few pictures for which technical details are given: 'Taken on Collodion August 30, 1855, clear with clouds floating before the sun; exposure eleven seconds; developed with pyrogallic acid.

Lens by Ross; focal length fifteen inches; diameter three inches; Diaphragm one inch.' Signed 'OGR Sept 1855'

BARNABY HAPPY c1854-6 RPS
Barnaby's enigmatic smile worried A. H. Wall:
'... with a crape hat-band, standing at what may be a ruin or a graveyard (I am afraid it may be the latter) there is a suggestiveness of widowerhood that so associated is almost cruel ...' (*Photographic News*, 10 June 1887)

'I PAYS!' c1854-6 GEH

'The man on the right is executing the privilege of every Englishman, "To grumble, and to pay"; but he is interrupted by the generosity of a man of the people, who is searching in his pocket for some money, crying "I pays".' (*Photographic Journal*, 15 Sept 1859)

Also reproduced by the Pretsch process in this number

OLD ENGLISH OAK   c1854-6   GCUT
'... the portrait of a jolly tar from Greenwich, hard, square, weather-beaten, and in every point a perfect model. He is drinking "The Queen! God bless her!"' (*Photographic News*, 2 Nov 1860)
Hard lighting is used for dramatic effect

CHARITY c1854-6 BCS

'Pointing to a group of children receiving fruit from a female in a doorway, Rejlander tells us how most photographers complain that all the heads are not equally sharp, and almost invariably point to some of the accessories as sadly out of focus, because he had taken some pains to throw them back into their proper place in the composition. "They think the head of the broom yonder ought to challenge attention as readily as the head of my principal model." ' (*Photographic News*, 26 Oct 1860)

49

D

OLD MAN AND SLEEPING CHILD c1854-6 EPS
This picture—whose title is missing—and PLAY (opposite) were evidently
intended as a pair. The stuffed dog makes regular appearances in Rejlander's
early genre

PLAY c1854-6 RPS

51

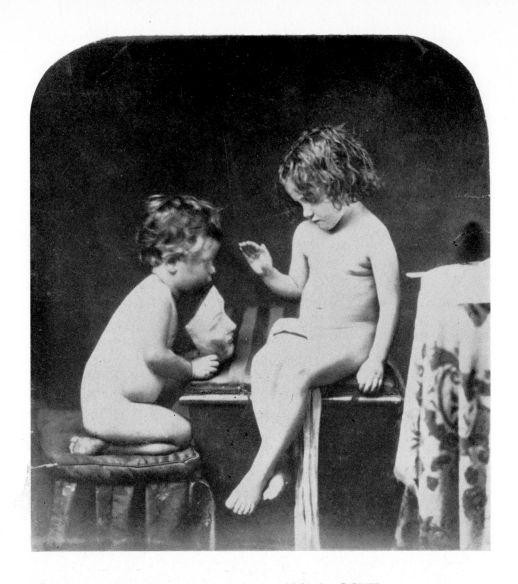

(*above*) CHILDREN PLAYING WITH A MASK   c1854-6   GCUT
The mask appears to cast a baleful influence over the children. Is this the recollection of a wall painting which Rejlander may have seen in Pompeii?

Opposite (*above left*) AFTER RAPHAEL'S SISTINE MADONNA   c1854-6   EPS
Rejlander believed that photography should teach artists the 'truth' about
anatomy, and he posed models in simulation of old masters to show (with respect)
where they were in error

(*above right*) FROM RAPHAEL'S SISTINE MADONNA, DRESDEN
(*from photogravure reproduction*)

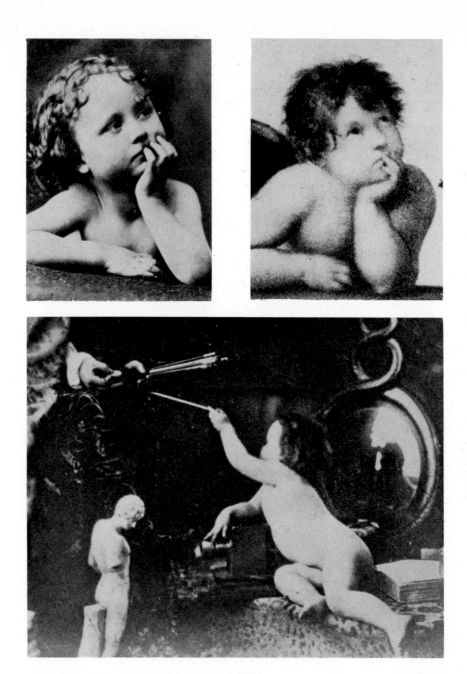

(*above*) INFANT PHOTOGRAPHY   c1856   EPS
'The hand of the artist holds many brushes; young photography—only a child—
gives him one more.' (*Photographic News*, 29 Oct 1875)
An essay in photographic allegory, INFANT ART, in which the same talented child
holds the palette and brush, is a companion piece

JUDITH AND HOLOFERNES c1856-7 EPS Composition
The Jewish heroine grasps the grisly printed-in head by the left ear. A critic
considered she was too good-natured looking to have been a murderess!

VIEWING A SPECTACLE (*probable title*) c1855-8 EPS Composition
Dress, drapes, and a printed-in fountain give a sophisticated air to this fashion-
plate of the 1850s

'DRAT THE EAST WIND!' c1856 RPS Composition

'... is worthy of Leech, though it merely represents the querulous distressed face of an old lady rubbing her rheumatic knees.' (*Journal of the Photographic Society of London*, 21 Jan 1857)

(*above and opposite*) CHARACTER STUDIES c1854-6   EPS
These studies were printed from parts of the original negatives, and were re-issued
by Rejlander during the 1860s as cartes-de-visite

REJLANDER AS DEMOCRITUS   c1865   GEH
Rejlander as the laughing philosopher. A pose probably inspired by an engraving which belonged to A. H. Wall. (*Illustrated Photographer*, Jan 1869)

SUMMER c1857 GCUT Composition?
Rejlander took many pictures of his wife, but never a better one than this. The
gesture, the Mona Lisa smile, the trees in their summer fulness—all create an
atmosphere of lightness and joy

NUDE STUDY c1857 GCUT
'Well, what is the suggestion here? Gross and indelicate? Anything at all like that created by a sight of those partially nude abominations now disgracing so many London shop windows? By jingo, I guess not!' (A. H. Wall, *Photographic News*, 2 Nov 1860)

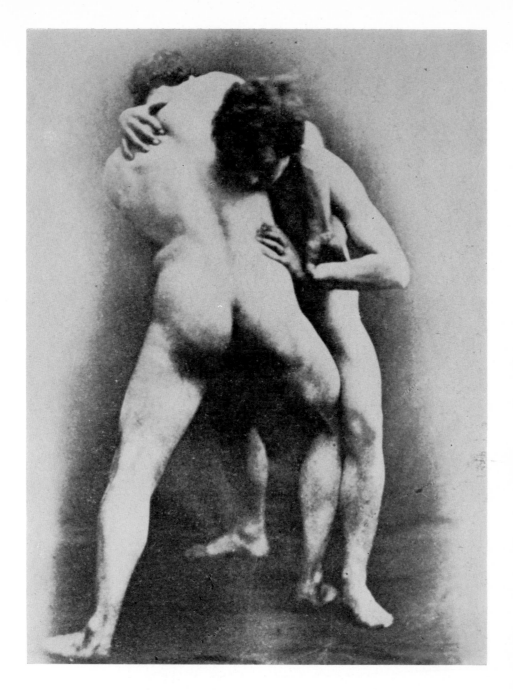

WRESTLING STUDY   1854-6   EPS
'... from the appearance of extreme action in certain muscles lasting not more than a few moments, the painter seldom succeeds in copying them so faithfully as they are given in such a photograph'. (A. H. Wall, *Photographic News,* 26 Oct 1860)

' 'TIS DARK WITHOUT, 'TIS LIGHT WITHIN'   c1855-60   GCUT

EVENING SUN c1860 ABB
There is a study of a model in classical garb shading her eyes which also bears
this title

JOHN COLEMAN AS *Belphegor* c1855 RPS
'... the itinerant actor of the French play, familiar to us in his striped trowsers, his lack-lustre eye, and sad and disappointed face, as he cuts away at the hard-earned loaf ...' (*Journal of the Photographic Society of London*, 21 Jan 1857)

PORTRAIT OF AN UNKNOWN MAN 1857 RPS

There is a similarity between this character and THE SAGE in THE TWO WAYS OF LIFE (version 2), though in that picture he wears a false beard. The technical details may be relevant to the studies in the composition:

'Taken on Collodion, March 22nd, 1857, late in the afternoon; weather, overcast, a gleam of yellow sunshine in the last second; Exposure twelve seconds; developed in Pyrogallic acid. Portrait Lens by Ross; focal length sixteen and three-quarters of an inch; diameter three and a quarter inches; Diaphragm one and three quarters of an inch.

Printed by the sun process by O. G. Rejlander'

E

THE SCRIPTURE READER 1858 EPS Composition
'The shelf with domestic utensils, and the German clock, with other accessories, render this a most inviting study. The grouping is excellent, and implies a master's hand.' (*Photographic Journal*, 1 Jan 1859)
But the critic overlooked the lack of coincidence of the floorboards!

'GOD SPEED HIM' 1858-9 EPS Composition

The fallen letter, the teacup tipped over, the interrupted darning, and the peasant woman's wrapped expression as her aged husband creaks hurriedly up the lane— suggest urgent tidings. A companion piece to THE WAYFARER

THE WAYFARER c1858-9 KM Composition
There are five printings: the dark bank, which shows evidence of sun-painting to deepen the tone; the old man with his bundle—probably a studio shot; the heap of stones at the left; a cluster of leaves; and the trees and country road in the distance

ALFRED LORD TENNYSON c1863-4 GCUT
'Most massive yet most delicate', wrote Thomas Carlyle, describing the poet's
features.
This portrait of Tennyson, sitting in his study chair, was taken in the porch at
Farringford, near Freshwater, Isle of Wight

LIONEL TENNYSON c1863-4 EPS
This was also taken at Farringford. Lionel was Tennyson's second son, born in 1854. He went away to school in the spring of 1864 when his curls were cut off, much against his mother's wish!

HALLAM TENNYSON c1863-4 ABB
Hallam was Tennyson's eldest son, born in 1852. He was named after his father's great friend and critic, Arthur Hallam
This set of phtographs of the Tennyson family was purchased by Lewis Carroll

'A PENNY PLEASE'   c1862-8   RPS
In those days Italian organ-grinders tramped the streets, churning out the familiar
tunes of Gounod and Verdi. The covering, half thrown back, was to suppress the
volume of the instrument

THE JUGGLER c1855-61 GEH
There is an illusion of movement created by the juggler's air of pleased surprise
as he watches the ball he is about to catch. The balls, needless to say, are sus-
pended from the ceiling

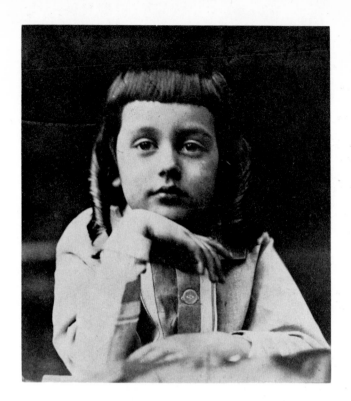

SEVERIN HOWER c1862-8 GEH
This sophisticated pose hardly tallies with the accepted image of the Victorian child. Little is known about Severin Hower, beyond the fact that he was an extremely photogenic child

'SHE'S LOOKING AT ME, THE DEAR CREATURE'
c1862-8
(*From half-tone reproduction*) 'The very idea of any "*dear creature*" looking even for a moment at such a hideous old rascal is highly ludicrous.'
(*British Journal of Photography*, 20 Nov 1868)

STUDY OF HANDS c1854 GCUT
Rejlander may have been the first photographer to specialise in details of the
human form, taken for the use of figure painters

YOUNG GIRL WEARING EMBROIDERED DRESS   c1866   ABB
The daughter of an Edinburgh publisher. A painting entitled FORGET-ME-NOT, closely based on Rejlander's photograph, was exhibited (without acknowledgement) at the Royal Academy. The girl's father was furious because the eyes were dark, whereas they should have been blue

FAMILY LIKENESS c1866-8 ABB
'How often, in a good photographic portrait, a family likeness to a relative is
discovered . . .' (H. P. Robinson, 1885)
Rejlander dressed and posed the child like her ancestress to put the matter of
family resemblance to the test

JOSEPH WILSON FOSTER   c1860   ABB
Probably taken at the Foster residence at Chorley, Lancashire, when Rejlander
was on his way to Scotland. The head resting on the arm was a device used in
preference to the head-rest

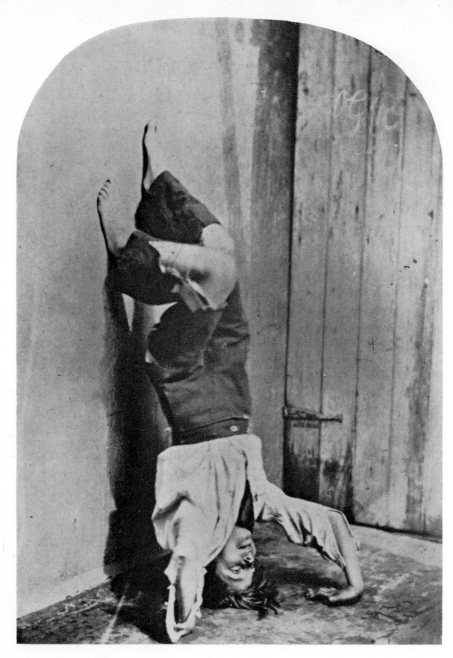

DAY IN TOWN c1860 GEH

'6 times for halfpeny' is chalked on the wall, and 'OGR' on the door at the right. This is the same sitter as in POOR JO

POOR JO c1860 GEH
Long after the photographer was forgotten, this picture continued to be used in charitable appeals. Actually, the rags do not stand close inspection: they are phoney

(above) ADDING INSULT TO INJURY   c1866-8   GCUT
A joke between a crossing-sweeper and a shoe-black

(*above*) 'LIGHTS, SIR?'   c1870   RPS
A natural and unselfconscious model, the match-seller stands at the entrance to the Albert Mansions studio

(*opposite right*) 'PLEASE GIVE US A COPPER'   c1866-8   GEH
A picture to emphasise the cock-sparrow cheeriness of the London crossing-sweeper; though no doubt there were exceptions

(*left*) 'JEM, IS IT A GOOD 'UN?'   c1866-8   GEH
Jem tests a halfpenny to make sure it is not counterfeit

F

A RAGGED-SCHOOL BOY   c1870   GEH
Probably the same urchin as on p81. He adopts a parody of the conventional
male pose

THE HEAD OF JOHN THE BAPTIST IN A CHARGER   c1857-8   RPS
Wall, while admiring the picture, noted a curious oversight—the jaw had not dropped. Rejlander, thanking him for this observation commented that this would have been fatal to the expression of holy resignation he had been anxious to secure. (*Photographic News*, 8 Oct 1886)
It was intended as part of a composition which never materialised, though SALOME was photographed at about the same period

AT THE CROSS   c1858   EPS
A study for a religious painting

WOMAN HOLDING A PAIR OF FEET   c1862-8   GEH
An enigma. The woman is 'Frizzlewig', who combined the duties of maidservant
and occasional model in the Rejlander household

PRAYER c1858-60 ABB
'. . . a beautiful and refined profile, with just that gentle curve of the short upper
lip which gives expression and appeal.' (A. H. Wall, *Photographic News*, 18 Feb
1887)

WINTER c1856-7 ABB
In pathetic contrast, this picture was originally exhibited together with SUMMER
(see p59), in which Mary Rejlander was the handsome model

THE GODDESS NICOTINA c1856-9 EPS
The earliest known example of anti-smoking propaganda. The allegory is explained by Rejlander's addiction to the weed

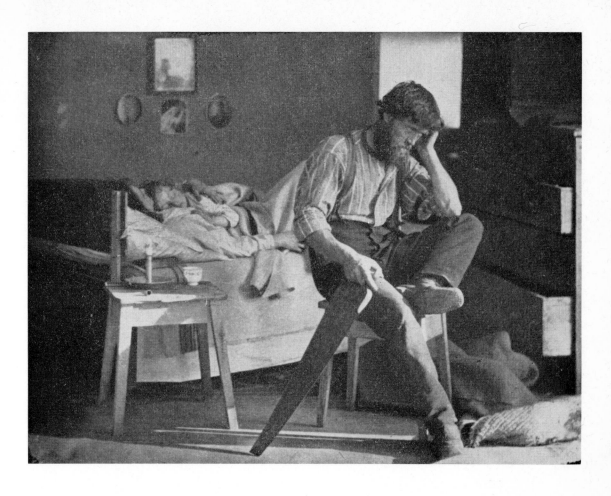

HARD TIMES c1860 RPS
The chest-of-drawers has been emptied in a futile search for anything worth
pawning.
A strange, re-posed version shows the carpenter with his wife and child super-
imposed upon a similar photograph, suggesting the grave thoughts which torture
the mind of a destitute man. (See *Life Library of Photography, Great Photographers*, 1971)

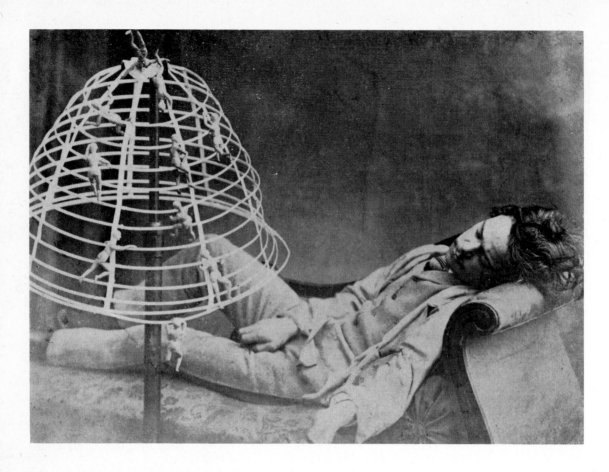

THE DREAM c1860 GEH
Jokes about the crinoline were all the rage, but this one has more subtlety. The tiny lay figures deride the somnolent bachelor, for soon he will be caught in the cage of matrimony. The engine of fashion menaces the sleeping figure

LEWIS CARROLL   28 March 1863   GCUT
Carroll's interest in photography began in 1855 when he was instructed in the
calotype by his uncle, Skeffington Lutwidge. In January 1857 he first saw and
admired Rejlander's studies of children, which undoubtedly influenced his own
style and technique

SHERRY COBBLER   c1868   GEH
Rejlander mixes himself a drink. An arsenic-impregnated fly-paper covers his
bald patch

REJLANDER AND THE GIPSY PEDLAR   c1862-8   GEH
Dialogue:
Gipsy woman (Mrs Rejlander), 'Buy a comb, sir?'
Rejlander, 'Can't you see, I'm bald'
Gipsy woman, offering a razor, 'You have a beard, sir!'

THE CHIMNEY SWEEP c1862-8 BCS
In this splendid study the sweep stands on the portable staircase leading down
to the tunnel studio, on which Rejlander was partial to posing his sitters

'DID SHE?'   c1862-8   ABB
An incident at the club re-enacted in the studio

1864 GCUT

'... the statuesque appearance of the drapery in GRIEF was finally secured after many efforts by using a thin fabric made to cling to the figure by being well damped.' (A. H. Wall, *Photographic News*, 31 Dec 1886)

(*left*) FLAMMA VESTALIS by Sir Edward Burne-Jones. (*From half-tone reproduction.*) The profile bears a close resemblance to that in Rejlander's TRULY THANKFUL

(*right*) TRULY THANKFUL   c1862-8   RPS

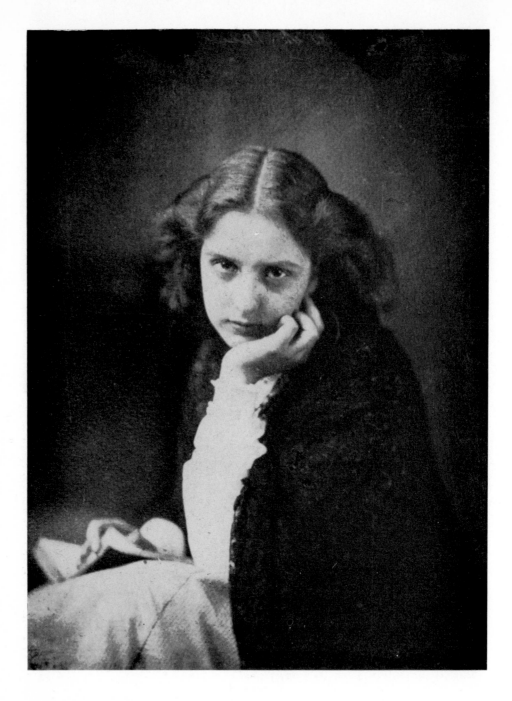

'IS IT TRUE?' c1862-8 RPS
Rejlander made many studies of this beautiful girl. The lighting from top and left is characteristic of the tunnel studio photographs

PATIENCE c1862-8 RPS
When exhibited, Rejlander appended the title: 'Let patience have her perfect work, St Paul.' The ascription being incorrect resulted in a polite exchange in the columns of *Photographic News*

HER PORTRAIT   c1862-8   GCUT
The title probably refers to the album on the girl's lap

YOUNG WOMAN WEARING WHITE, LOW-CUT DRESS   c1862-8   ABB
The title has been lost, but it could have been DESPONDENT

O.G.R. THE ARTIST INTRODUCES O.G.R. THE VOLUNTEER   c1871   RPS
Probably one of Rejlander's last efforts at double-printing. Taken at Albert
Mansions; the staircase was brought from the tunnel studio. Note that the picture
on the easel is GINX'S BABY (see p107)

REJLANDER AS GARIBALDI   c1862   RPS
Rejlander bore some resemblance to Garibaldi, whom he may have known

GUSTAVE DORÉ 1868 RPS
The most prolific, and the wealthiest, illustrator of his time—though not so successful as a painter. It is noteworthy, therefore, that as he lolls in an inspirational attitude he holds a palette and brushes

THE SOLAR CLUB   June? 1869   (*From heliotype reproduction*)

'...the only picture extant exhibiting so large a group of British photographers.'
(*Photographic Journal*, 8 Nov 1870)

The meetings of the Solar Club were both select and convivial. Founded by H. P. Robinson and G. Wharton Simpson, its members included many prominent photographers, some of whom made lasting contributions to the art and science of photography. The club's lighthearted rules prohibited members from wearing either court dress or dress suit 'unless they wish their portraits to hang up during every meeting as a warning to others'. Smoking was not forbidden; indeed, it was 'strictly enforced'.

In this group taken at the newly-opened studio in Albert Mansions, Victoria Street, the 'Chancellor', H. P. Robinson, is seated in the centre, while the smiling 'Vice-Chancellor', O. G. Rejlander, stands to his left. Beside these two pillars of Art Photography, there are others in the groups no less celebrated in their own fields:

William England, whose extensive tours for the London Stereoscopic Company first brought pictures of far-off places, in the startling realism of 3D, into the English drawing-room; his *America in the Stereoscope* (1859) being particularly popular.

Valentine Blanchard, pioneer of instantaneous photography. Early street photographs had an empty look, due to the long exposure. Blanchard went in amongst the traffic. Fitting up the interior of a cab as a darkroom, he made his exposures from the roof.

J. R. Johnson, of the Autotype Company, improved the carbon process; at that time the only method of producing permanent photographic prints.

George Wharton Simpson, editor of *Photographic News*, introduced collodio-chloride of silver printing paper, which was more sensitive, and more permanent than the customary albumen paper.

W. Mayland, noted for architectural photographs, some of which were exhibited in the United States in 1862. A specialist in ceramic photographs.

Cornelius Jabez Hughes had a lucrative business at Ryde, Isle of Wight, where has was also photographer to Queen Victoria. Began his photographic career as a daguerreotypist in 1845 with Mayall (also a member of the Solar Club). He had another establishment in London.

Russell Manners Gordon, FRGS; probably the only non-professional present.

John Werge, manager of Hughes' Oxford Street establishment. Employed in photography from its beginnings. Years later incorporated his recollections in *The Evolution of Photography* (1890).

Henry Baden Pritchard, superintendent of the photographic department, Woolwich Arsenal. Editor of *Photographic News* following the death of Wharton Simpson in 1880.

Walter B. Woodbury, inventor of the Woodburytype, one of the most successful of the early photomechanical processes.

105

Illustrations for Charles Darwin's *On the Expression of the Emotions in Man and Animals*, 1872 (From heliotype reproduction)

(*above left*) INDIGNATION
'Let it be observed how an indignant man ... holds his head erect, squares his shoulders and expands his chest'

(*above right*) DISGUST
'is generally accompanied by a frown, and often by gestures as if to push away or to guard against the offensive object'

(*left*) SURPRISE
'A surprised person often raises his open hands ... The flat palms are directed towards the person who causes this feeling, and the straightened fingers are separated'

'he bends his elbows closely inwards,
raises his open hands—the fingers separated. The head is often thrown a little on
one side; the eyebrows are elevated, and
this causes wrinkles across the forehead'

GINX'S BABY & CO   c1872
(*From half-tone reproduction*)
Rejlander laughs at himself. Who would have
dreamed that GINX'S BABY would have made him
solvent?

107

'SECOND EDITION!' 1871 GEH

One of Rejlander's finest genre studies. Babbage, inventor of the calculating machine, is dead—but the big news is Chicago's great fire, which broke out on Sunday 8 October 1871. The picture was exhibited in December of that year

HAPPY DAYS   c1872-3   RPS
Oscar and Mary re-live their courting days. Probably the last photograph of either
of them. Within a year Rejlander will be dying

REFERENCES

PROLOGUE
1 *British Journal of Photography* (16 Feb 1863)
2 *Household Words* (1853)
3 *A Catalogue of an Exhibition of Recent Specimens of photography exhibited at the Society of Arts, 18 John Street, Adelphi, in December 1852*
4 Ibid 1

WOLVERHAMPTON
1 *British Journal of Photography* (29 Jan 1875)
2 Personhistorisk Tidskrift, Stockholm (correspondence with the author)
3 Nymanson, S., Sundbyberg, Sweden (correspondence with the author)
4 Ibid 1
5 Lincoln Museum and Art Gallery, England
6 *The Photogram* (1894)
7 Ibid 1
8 *Photographic News* (18 Feb 1887)
9 *English Papier-Mâché* (1927?)
10 Royal Academy, London
11 Broadhurst, J. P. *In Memoriam William Parke*, Wolverhampton (1876)
12 'Bede, Cuthbert' (Rev Edward Bradley), *Photographic Pleasures* (1855)
13 *British Journal of Photography* (16 Feb 1863)
14 Ibid 10
15 Ibid 12
16 *Illustrated London News* (25 June 1853)
17 Jones, Joseph. *Historical Sketch of the Art and Literary Institutions of Wolverhampton, 1794-1897* (Wolverhampton, 1897)
18 *Wolverhampton Chronicle* (6 Aug 1856)
19 *Cosmos* (3 Oct 1856)
20 *Journal of the Photographic Society of London* (21 Jan 1857)
21 *Wolverhampton Chronicle* (14 Jan 1857)
22 *Photographic Notes* (15 April 1857)
23 *Photographic News* (18 Feb 1887)
24 *Photographic Notes* (1 July 1857)
25 *Journal of the Photographic Society of London* (21 Oct 1856)
26 Ibid 19
27 *Art Journal* (1856)
28 Ibid 12
29 Ibid 19
30 *Wolverhampton Chronicle* (24 Sept 1856)
31 Ibid 19
32 Ibid 19
33 Ibid 19
34 Coleman, J. *Fifty Years of an Actor's Life* (1904)
35 *Photographic Journal* (Sept 1855)
36 *Photographic Notes* (15 Oct 1856)
37 *Photographic News* (30 July 1886)
38 *Wolverhampton Chronicle* (15 April 1857)
39 *British Journal of Photography* (2 Mar 1863)
40 *Photographic Notes* (15 July 1857)
41 *Athenaeum* (25 April 1857)
42 *Photographic Notes* (28 April 1857)
43 *Liverpool and Manchester Photographic Journal* (May 1857)
44 Ibid 43
45 *Photographic Journal* (April 1938)
46 *British Journal of Photography* (15 Oct 1863)
47 *Journal of the Photographic Society of London* (21 April 1858)
48 Ibid 47
49 Ibid 47
50 Gernsheim, A. and H. *History of Photography* (1955)
51 Ibid 45
52 Ibid 50
53 Werge, J. *The Evolution of Photography* (1890)
54 *Pictorial Times* (27 Apr 1847)
55 Farr, D. *William Etty* (1958)
56 Rossetti, W. M. *Pre-Raphaelite Diaries and Letters* (1902?)
57 Jones, James P. *Wolverhampton Journal* (Mar 1908)
58 Wolverhampton Public Library Collection
59 *Art Journal* (1858)
60 *Journal of the Photographic Society of London* (21 May 1858)
61 *Photographic Notes* (1 Jan 1858)
62 Ibid 47
63 *Photographic Journal* (1 Jan 1859)
64 Robinson, H. P. *The Elements of a Pictorial Photograph* (1896)
65 *American Journal of Photography* (1862)
66 *Photographic News* (11 Mar 1859)
67 *Practical Photography* (1895)
68 *Photographic Notes* (15 Jan 1863)

69 *Photographic Notes* (1 Mar 1863)
70 *Photographic News* (31 Oct 1862)
71 Ibid 57
72 *Photographic News* (26 Oct 1860)
73 Ibid 55
74 Ibid 72
75 Ibid 47
76 Ibid 47
77 Darwin, Charles, FRS. *On the Expression of the Emotions in Man and Animals* (1872)
78 Ibid 72 and 2 Nov 1860
79 Wymer, N. *Father of Nobody's Children* (1954)
80 *British Journal of Photography* (5 Jan 1861)
81 Ibid 57

MALDEN ROAD
 1 London Business Directory 1862
 2 *Photographic News* (2 Sept 1887)
 3 *Photographic News* (6 Mar 1863)
 4 *Photographic News* (2 April 1863)
 5 *Photographic News* (4 Mar 1864)
 6 *Photographic News* (11 Mar 1864)
 7 Green, R. L. *The Diaries of Lewis Carroll* (1953)
 8 Gernsheim, H. *Lewis Carroll—Photographer* (1949)
 9 *Photographic News* (27 Aug 1886)
10 *Photographic News* (3 Sept 1886)
11 *Illustrated Photographer* (30 Oct 1868)
12 *Photographic News* (24 Sept 1886)
13 *Photographic News* (10 June 1887)
14 *British Journal of Photography* (1 Feb 1864)
15 *The Photogram* (1894)
16 *British Journal of Photography* (27 July 1864)
17 *British Journal of Photography* (9 Sept 1864)
18 Ibid 17
19 *Photographische Mittheilungen* (June 1865)
20 Ibid 19

21 *British Journal of Photography* (5 Oct 1866)
22 *British Journal of Photography* (July 1866)
23 *Photographic News* (8 Oct 1886)
24 *British Journal of Photography* (16 Mar 1866)
25 *Photographic Notes* (1864)
26 *British Journal of Photography* (Oct 1866)
27 *British Journal of Photography Almanac* (1866)
28 *Photographic News* (18 Feb 1887)
29 *British Journal of Photography* (20 Nov 1868)
30 *Art Journal* (1869)
31 *Art Journal* (1868)
32 *Illustrated Photographer* (27 Nov 1868)
33 *Illustrated Photographer* (16 Apr 1869)

ALBERT MANSIONS
 1 *Philadelphia Photographer* (1869)
 2 *Illustrated Photographer* (28 May 1869)
 3 *Illustrated Photographer* (18 June 1869)
 4 *British Journal of Photography Almanac* (1870)
 5 *British Journal of Photography Almanac* (1872)
 6 Darwin, Charles, FRS. *On the Expression of the Emotions in Man and Animals* (1872)
 7 *Photographic News* (3 Jan 1890)
 8 *Photographische Rundschau* (1901)
 9 *Photographic News* (2 July 1875)
10 Artists Rifles Association rolls, London
11 *British Journal of Photography Almanac* (1881)
12 Ibid 7
13 *Photographic News* (2 April 1875)
14 *Photographic News* (22 Jan 1875)
15 *British Journal of Photography* (29 Jan 1875)
16 Ibid 15
17 *American Amateur Photographer* (1890)
18 *The Photogram* (1894)
19 *Camera Obscura* (Feb 1901)
20 *Photographic News* (18 Feb 1887)
21 *Philadelphia Photographer* (1875)

ACKNOWLEDGEMENTS

I am greatly indebted to the following persons and institutions who, by granting me permission to reproduce from a selection of their photographs by Rejlander, or by suggesting references, answering enquiries, or providing facilities, have made it possible for me to compile this book:

Dr A. Beryl Beakbane; Birmingham Art Gallery and Public Libraries; Mr H. T. Bolus, Birmingham Photographic Society; British Museum Newspaper Library; Herr Jöran Cassel, President Swedish Photographers Association; City of Lincoln Public Library; Mr P. B. Cowell, Honorary Secretary Artist Rifles Association; Mr Arthur Dalladay, former editor British Journal of Photography; Mr Peter Davies; Mr F. Band and Mr Robert M. Strathdee, Edinburgh Photographic Society; Mr J. Clement Jones, editor, and library staff of the *Express and Star,* Wolverhampton; Herr Pär Frank, Secretary Friends of the Photographic Museum, Stockholm; Greater London Council, Street Naming Department; Herr Carl Gullers; Herr Per Hemmingsson; Herr Bertil Janson; Dr Birgitta Lager, Personhistorisk Tidskrift, Stockholm; Lambeth Public Libraries; Colonel W. G. McHardy, MBE, MC, Resident Factor, Balmoral Castle; Mr David McNamara; Sir Charles Mander, Bt; Mr H. J. Malyon, Secretary General Cemetery Co, Kensal Green; Manchester Public Library; Mr John W. Meaney, Curator Gernsheim Collection, University of Texas; Mr Beaumont Newhall, former director George Eastman House, Rochester, NY; New York Public Library; Royal Academy of Arts, London; Principal Probate Registry, Somerset House, London; Public Records Office, London; Miss Sybil Rosenfeld, Secretary Society for Theatre Research, London; Mr Arthur T. Gill, Mr L. E. Hallet, OBE, former secretary, Mrs F. Johnston, and the late R. C. Leighton Herdson, Royal Photographic Society; the late Dr R. S. Schultze, Curator Kodak Museum, Harrow; Miss A. Scott-Elliot, MVO, Keeper of Prints and Drawings, Windsor; Intendent Åke Sidwall, Fotografiska Museet, Stockholm; the Simon Community, Malden Road, London; Herr Lars-G. Warne, Swedish Institute for Cultural Relations, London; Sir Charles Tennyson, CMG; Herr S. Nymanson; Mr John Underwood; Mr C. H. Gibbs-Smith, Keeper of Department of Public Relations and Education, Mr John P. Harthan, Keeper of the Library, and Mr John F. Physick, Victoria and Albert Museum; Westminster Public Library; Mr W. G. Meredith, Wolverhampton Borough Engineer's Department; Mr F. Mason and staff, Wolverhampton Public Library.

Permission to reproduce from Charles Darwin's *On the Expression of the Emotions in Man and Animals* has been courteously granted by John Murray (Publishers) Ltd.

The quotations from *The Diaries of Lewis Carroll,* edited by Roger Lancelyn Green, published by Cassell & Co, are reproduced by kind permission of the estate of Lewis Carroll, and Roger Lancelyn Green.